THERE IS HOPE

by ELWOOD MC QUAID

The Friends of Israel Gospel Ministry, Inc.
P. O. Box 908, Bellmawr, NJ 08099

THERE IS HOPE

All rights reserved
Printed in the United States of America
Library of Congress Catalog Card Number: 96-84010
ISBN 0-915540-11-8

The Friends of Israel Gospel Ministry, Inc.
P. O. Box 908, Bellmawr, New Jersey 08099

TABLE OF CONTENTS

DEDICATION

For Maxine, whose love of the "blessed hope"
has been her constant companion.

INTRODUCTION

The old cultist huffed and puffed for what seemed to be the greater part of an hour.

It was late at night. My only companions were the flipping, broken white lines on the highway brought into view by my car's headlights. For me, long road trips produce acute boredom that is sometimes eased by relentlessly turning the radio dial in mostly fruitless pursuits of something worth listening to.

It was his voice that caused me to stop chasing stations and listen to what he had to say. The pseudo-Bible expositor spoke of personal revelations and insights previously unknown to run-of-the-mill preachers. His mission was to deliver benighted souls from the clutches of such ministerial types, who were given to traditional, conservative Bible teaching. His was a "special" word that would open new vistas of understanding to those who would follow him and his teachings. His delivery had a sort of "wipe out the opposition" air of authority, and it was obvious that he had oratorical abilities that would draw many to him—not by what he said but by the way in which he said it.

When the program was over, I turned off the radio and attempted to analyze what the man had said. I could not remember anything that was biblically or logically coherent. In other words, the cult leader had said nothing. But he had said nothing as well as I had ever heard it said.

Which brings me to the reason I am writing this book. We are today beset by throngs of self-ordained authorities who are bombarding us with their particular brands of insights and revelations hot off the wire, some claim, from God Himself. This seems especially true in matters related to end-time events, the Rapture of the church, and the Lord's second advent. Most of these people are not as out of touch with biblical reality as the oratorical spellbinder I heard on the radio that night. Nevertheless, there is a great deal of confusion developing today about prophecy and how we are to interpret it and respond to what is taking place in these last days. Some people are disoriented, poorly taught, or misled to the point that they have thrown up their hands and want nothing to do with prophecy and matters related to the Second Coming. "After all," some are telling us, "who really knows anyway? I'll just wait and see what happens."

Such attitudes are in direct contradiction to what we are taught in the Word of God. Believers are to be *people of the hope*—the "blessed hope" of the coming of the Savior to call us home. Being robbed of or confused about that hope creates Christians with deficiencies in an area that is fundamental to our faith.

Fully one-third of the Bible relates to prophecy and end-time events. It is therefore reasonable to assume that if God thought it important enough to give so much space to the subject, we must take what He has to say seriously and seek to apply prophetic truth to our lives in intensely personal ways.

My object in writing this book is twofold: certainty and simplicity. Certainty because, in a world moving perilously close to the brink of chaos, THERE IS HOPE—a hope that is available only in Christ. In Him there is the certainty of everlasting life and the certainty of His presence—which is, of course, integrally related to the promise that He will return and call us to Himself.

Also, this book is about simplicity. I firmly believe that the things that are most essential to our lives and well-being as Christians are addressed by an understanding Lord in simple terms. Granted, there are some matters in Scripture that are, as Peter said of some of Paul's writings, "hard to be understood" (2 Peter 3:16). We can all be thankful for accomplished, godly theologians who can dig skillfully into the deep things of God and bring us needed light. But when it comes to subjects of monumental importance, such as salvation and the Second Coming, God places essential elements of truth on a level easy to reach— a plane where the simplest among us does not need hidden keys or maze-like, meandering interpretations to find what we need most. God is not of a mind to hide things from us, but to reveal them to us. The very title of the Book of the Revelation is proof of this. It is a God-given revelation. He wants us to know!

We understand that for those people who have developed considerable expertise in obscuring the obvious, simplicity does not set well. However, those of us in need of "truth made plain" can appreciate the fact that He understands us and has provided in advance just what we need.

—EMQ

Christ's return is always imminent; we must never cease to watch for it. The first Christians thought it so near that they faced the possibility of Jesus' return in their lifetime. Paul thinks he too may perhaps be alive when it happens.

—Gaston Deluz

Chapter One

SOMETHING FOR
YOUR HEART

The cemetery was bitterly cold that day. Several inches of snow covered the ground and was being whipped around the open grave by aggressive gusts of wind. Because a grief-stricken mother could not bear the thought of parting with the body of her infant daughter, she insisted that the tiny coffin be opened one last time.

As a minister, I have officiated at scores of funerals. Details of most of them are blurred in my memory or completely forgotten. But this one refuses to be erased. After nearly two decades, the heartrending picture still from time to time

appears vividly before me. Seeing devastated young parents
on their knees looking into the tiny face of one too soon gone,
as a cruel winter wind ruffled the white satin dress she wore, is
not something I care to remember. Frankly, it was a scene that,
to my mind, after all of these years, is still incomprehensible.
No studied explanation of medical data or questions of
unpleasant alternatives, had she survived, will suffice. A child
had died and been buried at the worst of times—from a strict-
ly human point of view, it defies rational explanation.

Be Not Troubled

In some measure, we can compare the devastated emotions of the parents described above to Jesus' disciples when
He made the stunning announcement that He was about to
leave them. "One of you shall betray me," Jesus told them
in the upper room (John 13:21). "Little children," He went
on to say, "yet a little while I am with you. Ye shall seek
me; and as I said unto the Jews, Where I go, ye cannot
come; so now I say unto you" (John 13:33). At the heart of
it all was His word to them that He was going up to
Jerusalem, not to take His throne and establish the millennial kingdom they looked and longed for, but to die.

> And Jesus, going up to Jerusalem, took the
> twelve disciples aside along the way, and said
> unto them, Behold, we go up to Jerusalem;
> and the Son of man shall be betrayed unto the
> chief priests and unto the scribes, and they
> shall condemn him to death, And shall deliv-
> er him to the Gentiles to mock, and to

scourge, and to crucify him. And the third
day he shall rise again (Matthew 20:17-19).
He had told them this from time to time. His death was
a necessity. It would, in fact, be the direct fulfillment of
Isaiah 53.

"For I say unto you that this that is written must yet be
accomplished in me, *And he was reckoned among the trans-
gressors* [Isaiah 53:12]; for the things concerning me have a
fulfillment" (Luke 22:37, italics added).

There is a rather intriguing verse that helps to explain why
the disciples were so dull of ear when Jesus made statements
about His impending death. *"And they understood none of
these things; and this saying was hidden from them, neither
knew they the things which were spoken"* (Luke 18:34).

The disciples did not hear what He was saying for two
reasons.

First, it obviously was not the right time for them to fully
comprehend what would take place in Jerusalem; that truth was
divinely hidden from them for a time.

Then, and more to the point of what we need to learn, they
were guilty of selective hearing. Rather like our children,
Jesus' disciples were listening for what they wanted to hear.

What was that?

It was those things that Jesus was teaching them regarding
the coming kingdom. We can well imagine, as He stood before
the multitudes instructing them in those essential elements of
God's plan for the nation, that they sketched in their minds
plans for kingdom palaces. Their comprehension focused on
the fact that one day the Messiah would come, triumph over
their oppressors, and take His throne. These men we know as
Jesus' disciples were sure that when that day came, they would

reign with Him. Can they be faulted for listening more intent-
ly to those instructions related to the kingdom?

In a sense, yes. They could not say that they had not
been forewarned. Neither could they claim that they were
not prepared.

However, when the time came for them to face His death,
they were as unprepared as we often are when facing the death
of a loved one or some unexpected or unexplained tragedy.

His most intimate followers, men who with but one excep-
tion loved Him dearly, were crushed when word of His death
finally got through to them. When the event actually took
place, they scattered and hid themselves like fugitives on the
brink of losing their lives.

But He had prepared them, and later His words would burn
in their hearts.

Jesus had, in fact, foreseen their devastated state and given
them their answer in *certain* and *simple* terms.

A Matter of the Heart

Their need at that decisive moment was not an extended
lecture in the theology of the coming church age and the
delay of the kingdom. Their minds were too depressed to
process such information, as important as it may have
been. They were sick at heart. He was leaving them.
They had put their unqualified trust in Him, and now they
were to be left alone.

Why?

At that moment the pressing need was not for an explanation but rather for a declaration of intention. Jesus was

about to say something they could hang their hearts on. Although it would be some time before they would begin to grasp, as the Spirit taught them, what Calvary was really all about, He was delivering something that would carry them through the fury of the storm that was about to break upon them.

His words lay bare the heart of this book. There are times that are most certainly times of the heart—times when we as believers need the comfort that only certainty, simply framed, can give.

Let's examine what He said and see the pattern for our hope unveiled.

> *Let not your heart be troubled; ye believe in God, believe also in me. In my Father's house are many mansions; if it were not so, I would have told you. I go to prepare a place for you. And if I go and prepare a place for you, I will come again, and receive you unto myself, that where I am, there ye may be also. And where I go ye know, and the way ye know. Thomas saith unto him, Lord, we know not where thou goest; and how can we know the way? Jesus saith unto him, I am the way, the truth, and the life; no man cometh unto the Father, but by me* (John 14:1-6).

Looking Toward a New Age

The disciples were standing with Jesus on the verge of a completely new age (dispensation). They had been taught

things pertaining to the kingdom age. But with His announcement that He was going away, that promised literal and historical kingdom would be postponed.

This is verified in Acts 1:6-7. After His death and resurrection, and on the verge of His ascension into heaven, the disciples posed a question to Him: "Lord, wilt thou at this time
restore again the kingdom to Israel? And he said unto them, It
is not for you to know the times or the seasons, which the
Father hath put in his own power."

Those people who today are attempting to date the Lord's
return would be well advised to hear what He told His followers two millennia ago: *"It is not for you to know the times or
the seasons...."* Case closed! The kingdom had not been done
away with. It would most assuredly come. But in the interim,
they and we are committed to another commission in, if you
will, a completely new age—the age of grace.

Believers were to be wonderfully equipped for the time
when Christ would be physically absent from His earthbound
church. In John 14 through 16, He described the dimensions
of the provision He would leave at their disposal.

• He will be listening and prepared to take every request to the
  Father. "If ye shall ask anything in my name, I will do it"
  (John 14:14).

• He would send them another Comforter, the Holy Spirit, to
  take up residence within the very believers He would soon
  be parted from. "And I will pray the Father, and he shall give
  you another Comforter, that he may abide with you forever"
  (John 14:16).

• He revealed the Comforter's ministry to and through believers:
     * "He shall teach you all things" (John 14:26).
     * "And bring all things to your remembrance, whatever I

have said unto you" (John 14:26).
* "He shall testify of me" (John 15:26).
* "And ye [through the Spirit's enabling] also shall bear witness" (John 15:27).
* "He will reprove the world of sin, and of righteousness, and of judgment (John 16:8).
* "He will guide you into all truth" (John 16:13).
* "He will show you things to come" (John 16:13).
* "He shall glorify me" (John 16:14).
* "He shall take of mine [the things of Christ], and shall show it unto you" (John 16:15).
• Finally, He assured them that through His provision they could be counted among the overcomers. "These things I have spoken unto you, that in me ye might have peace. In the world ye shall have tribulation: but be of good cheer; I have overcome the world" (John 16:33).

Meeting the "Now" Need

His preface to the soon-to-be-realized fruits of the new age was to address the need that was stunning their minds and numbing their hearts at that crucial moment. They needed a "right now" source of comfort and assurance.

His first word to them was, *"Let not your heart be troubled."* It was coupled with an indispensable proposition: *"Ye believe in God, believe also in me"* (John 14:1).

Believe was to be the watchword of the new age of grace that was to come. Soon He would make the last sacrifice ever necessary to redeem humanity. In a very real sense, the fire was dying on Israel's grand sacrificial altar. No longer would

annual pilgrimages to the Temple Mount be an integral part of
the divine program. The old was passing away. A new order
was upon them.

The thrust of what was dawning is set forth magnifi-
cently in the Book of Acts. Paul and Silas, deep in the
bowels of the jail at Philippi, sang praise to God as a pre-
lude to a nerve-shattering earthquake. The jailer, first
thinking that the prisoners had escaped, was ready to fall
upon his own sword rather than face the wrath of his supe-
riors. "Do thyself no harm," Paul cried, "for we are all
here." And then the trembling jailer, with a question on his
lips, brought them out. "Sirs," he said, "what must I do to
be saved?"

The apostle's response was simple: *"Believe on the Lord
Jesus Christ, and thou shalt be saved, and thy house"* (Acts
16:25-34).

Here is profound certainty in simplicity. Believe!
Believe! Believe! Jesus has indeed paid it all. Believe and
be saved.

The Father's House

*"In my Father's house are many mansions; if it were not so,
I would have told you"* (John 14:2).

The security of being assured of a dwelling place in "the
city of God" causes the darkest clouds to flee away. The
mansions in glory are rightly the stuff of the songs of the
redeemed. What better way to celebrate our future destiny? Our faces are set toward home, and one day—

whether we collectively flee away to Him or slip out of this world through death's door one by one—"we have a building of God, an house not made with hands, eternal in the heavens" (2 Corinthians 5:1).

Some rather tongue-in-cheek disputes go on between students of Scripture regarding our heavenly home. Some sing of their readiness to settle for "a little cabin in the corner of glory land," a prospect held in ridicule by many of their peers. Then there are those who relish the thought of mansions like sprawling Roman villas covering vast expanses of heavenly real estate. Somewhere in between are those people—ever cautious of encouraging a thirst for the opulent or, on the other hand, a miserly view of what the Lord plans for His children—who seem fond of referring to our mansions as rooms. They seem to be saying, "Don't get too excited; a room will do." Well, yes, I suppose a room will do—if that is what He plans. But it really doesn't make a bit of difference whether it is a mansion, a room, or a cabin. You see, we know the architect. If Jesus is preparing us a house, as He promised, we need not worry about its dimensions or decorations. All will be well prepared by the time we take up occupancy.

There is a marvelous account of God's care for His people in Ezekiel 11:16. At that time Israel was scattered and suffering, bearing the inevitable consequences of wandering from the will of God. In spite of all of this, God assured them, *"Although I have cast them far off among the nations, and although I have scattered them among the countries, yet will I be to them a little sanctuary in the countries where they shall come."*

Sanctuary—here it is likened to a place of asylum, a God-given hiding place for a people He calls "chosen." In spite of themselves, the Lord of glory pledges Himself to their protection. They will, as a nation, survive.

How much more wonderful it is to contemplate that this same God, ever faithful to His Word, is preparing, through His Son, our eternal home.

I Will Come Again

Whatever the disciples may have thought at the moment, their Lord was not deserting them. Nor was He being so victimized by His enemies that He was more concerned about His own suffering than about their future welfare. The cross was not going to be a terminal event. It was simply one stage of a program that would secure the promise of a permanent relationship.

"And if I go and prepare a place for you, I will come again, and receive you unto myself, that where I am, there ye may be also" (John 14:3).

With these transcending words, we are introduced to the concept of the Rapture of the church. The Rapture is a clear departure from the Lord's teaching about the second advent coming of Christ, in which He will set up His kingdom and rule over reconciled Israel for a full thousand years. As we shall see, that coming will bring Him back to the city of Jerusalem, where He will take His seat of regal authority upon the throne of David.

The coming promised to believers in John 14 is a distinct departure from the Second Coming concept. Most noteworthy is that in this coming He promised that there will be a day when He will come in the clouds to call believers up to heaven. The Rapture scenario is described in intricate detail in the Book of First Thessalonians (a passage we will explore fully later). Now however it is important to understand that what Jesus told His followers here is not what He had been teaching them concerning the kingdom.

Proof of this is found in the statement, "where I am, there ye may be also." Jesus is preparing a wonderful place in the heavens, and when the time is right He will come for His church and take His people home. This is the grand event that is properly known as the "blessed hope." It is the certainty that at any moment we may be called away and be found with Him.

A logical question was raised by Thomas, otherwise known as "the doubter": *"Lord, we know not where thou goest; and how can we know the way?"* (John 14:5) His was a question we might well expect from one who had just been told that his beloved Master was leaving to move toward some obscure place in the heavens. Jesus' response was sublime.

"Jesus saith unto him, I am the way, the truth, and the life; no man cometh unto the Father, but by me" (John 14:6).

Let's reconstruct what the Lord told His stricken disciples who desperately needed something for their hearts.

- He told them to *believe*, to trust Him as personal Savior and Lord. In so doing, they would indeed find the way home.
- Although He was to be separated from them physically for a time, they need not worry. He was preparing a place for them in heaven.
- He promised that one day He would come again and call them home.

- They would thereafter never be parted from Him again. Here is a wonder of simplicity that only a sovereign and caring Lord could bring together. I think we can properly say that God brought *Him* (Jesus), *heaven*, and *home* together in a way that would provide every generation of future believers a hope to hang their hearts on.

Maranatha

At precisely this juncture in Scripture, God chose to implant the pulsing *Maranatha* hope into the anatomy of His church. From the moment of Jesus' departure from the Mount of Olives in Jerusalem, *Maranatha* (*Our Lord, come!*) became the watchword of the church. It was their greeting and parting word of hope. Perhaps He would come for them today.

I was speaking at a church in the Midwest some time ago. My topic was the Rapture and the imminent return of Christ. As I stood in the foyer greeting worshipers following the service, a woman walked up to me, extended her hand, said "Maranatha," and without another word left the building.

What a thrilling way, I thought, to close a service on the Rapture. Two thousand years and thousands of miles removed from the place where the word was coined, believers are still greeting one another with this singular word of hope and expectation.

Where is the Promise of His Coming?

In spite of His clear promise and the obvious response of the early church, we can anticipate a chorus of voices saying that there is no word of hope coming from the Scriptures declaring an imminent return of Christ for His saints. In spite of the fact that we have just considered one such word, and the fact that the early church believed they would experience the Rapture in their lifetimes, some believers still strenuously object to this hope.

Such objections are anticipated in the Word of God.

"Knowing this first, that there shall come in the last days scoffers, walking after their own lusts, And saying, Where is the promise of his coming? For since the fathers fell asleep, all things continue as they were from the beginning of the creation" (2 Peter 3:3-4).

The attack being directed at the prospect of the Second Coming that Peter promised for the last days is not a casual theological difference of opinion. Actually, it calls into question the very truthfulness and integrity of the one who made the promise—Jesus Christ.

The phrase "Where is the promise of His coming?" is also properly rendered, as it is in the New International Version, "Where is this 'coming' he promised?" Jesus is the one who promised to return. In John 14 it relates directly to His coming to Rapture His church. Thus, the reliability of Christ Himself is being called into question.

We need not be surprised when some people boldly deny the coming of the Lord or others offer sometimes bizarre alternatives.

Among the novel and, yes, even bizarre teachings being floated today are those claiming to have discovered the day of the Lord's return. For the last decade there has been a substantial increase in the number of theories claiming to have uncovered the secret key to determining the exact time of the Lord's return. And we can be assured that as we approach the year 2000, the phenomenon will not diminish. There will be an increase in the number of prophetic "experts" claiming to know "the day and the hour" of His appearing.

Some people act as though this is a kind of Bible trivia guessing game in which no harm is done, and perhaps we even garner some good by causing people to think of the Lord's coming. This is not true. Several rather serious problems attach themselves to the folly of date setting.

First, it is something that the Lord has warned us not to do.

"But of that day and that hour knoweth no man, no, not the angels in heaven, neither the Son, but the Father. Take heed, watch and pray; for ye know not when the time is" (Mark 13:32-33).

Then there is the matter of distracting people from carrying out their commission. Often people get so caught up in some self-proclaimed "insider's" teaching on the Rapture or Second Coming that they neglect the responsibility to evangelize. Many become more concerned about converting believers to their particular view than reaching the lost with the gospel.

Inevitably, when the date set for the Rapture or Second Coming passes—and for nearly two thousand years it always has—those espousing the view are humiliated, often ridiculed, and their confidence in the Bible is shaken.

A number of such examples can be mentioned. Of particular notoriety was the book setting forth 88 reasons why the Rapture would take place in September of 1988. September (which seems to be a favorite month of date setters) came and went—nothing happened. The resourceful author was not stymied; he claimed to have been one year off in his calculations and went back to the drawing board. Then he found 89 reasons why the event would assuredly occur in 1989. Although the book caused quite a stir for a time—until October of '89 as I recall—and reportedly sold some 4 million copies, the whole theory toppled with the passing of the date.

While the credulous waited for the next person with special revelation from God to appear on the scene, many more thoughtful brethren began to wonder whether talking about the Lord's coming was more of a hindrance than a help to the cause of Christ.

But the worst of these encounters is seen in the reaction of unbelievers toward the apparent failure of God to take heed when He is commanded to meet a particular date set by someone fancying himself an expert in such things. In their minds, these failures confirm the reason for their continued unbelief and give rise to suspicions about anyone's ability, or sincerity for that matter, to rightly divide the Word of God.

Are all such people charlatans looking for financial gain or personal aggrandizement? Some, perhaps many, are. But not all. There are among them a host of sincere people who are victims and therefore victimize others because they have never learned how to rightly divide the Word of God. Given the slippage in sound Bible teaching that we are witnessing today, we cannot be overly optimistic that matters will improve.

Nevertheless, it is incumbent on all believers to learn how to study the Scriptures as they were meant to be interpreted.

Once again, such study and subsequent knowledge are not beyond the reach of the average Christian.

It is of utmost importance to realize that within the confines of the Bible, God has told us all that we need to know. Second Peter 1 makes this clear.

> According as his divine power hath given unto us all things that pertain unto life and god-liness, *through the knowledge of him* that hath called us to glory and virtue; By which are given unto us exceedingly great and precious promis-es, that by these ye might be partakers of the divine nature, having escaped the corruption that is in the world through lust (vv. 3-4).

The "knowledge" spoken of here is the understanding that comes to us through the written Word of God and implies "the full knowledge" of God. All of the available knowledge that He has provided in matters pertaining to life and godliness has been transmitted to us through His Word. Therefore, the best defense against error is to become an able student of the Scriptures

So many believers are confused and consequently confusing others about the Rapture and Second Coming of Christ because of a basic inadequacy in respecting the central divisions of the Scriptures established by God and identified for our instruction and edification.

The Scripture has left the whole matter, as far as I can see, with an intentional indistinctness, that we may be always expecting Christ to come, and that we may be watching for His coming at any hour and every hour....He will come in His own time, and we are always to be looking for His appearing.

—Charles Haddon Spurgeon

Chapter Two

DRAWING THE
BOTTOM LINES

The man was a doctor, well dressed, articulate, and very angry. Red-faced, he leveled a withering assault against much of what I had said to the congregation. The occasion was a Bible conference. I had been asked to speak on Bible prophecy, especially as it relates to Israel. In the main, my message dealt with the four phases of God's program for Israel and the Jewish people.

His heated objections roughly followed two lines. First, Jewish people were responsible for virtually every evil visited upon humanity. Not being Jewish myself, speaking of them in a positive light made me a traitor to my own people. Second, he was a Gentile involved in a group now distinguishing itself as the true Israel of God—spiritual preemptors of the promises given by God to Abraham. Jewish people were no longer worthy of the covenant promises, which had now been rescinded and bestowed upon the true Israel—him and his cohorts. All that was left to Jewry were the curses that, in his mind, they so richly deserved.

The man's attitude was a visual demonstration of how the sense and actual sentences of God's Word can be perverted and manipulated to afflict those people deemed undesirable. At the same time, it can be used to falsely establish claims of superiority. It also points up the danger of not understanding basic elements of teaching that come to us from the Bible.

Believers are admonished, as was young Timothy, to be diligent students of the Word of God. "Study," he was told, "to show thyself approved unto God, a workman that needeth not to be ashamed, rightly dividing the word of truth" (2 Timothy 2:15).

A concise passage in 1 Corinthians 10 sheds light on precisely how the Scriptures are to be *rightly divided*. First, we find an admonition to be godly. *"Whether, therefore, ye eat, or drink, or whatever ye do, do all to the glory of God"* (v. 31). So doing produces an inevitable testimony. It is with this in mind that the next verse is directed.

"Give no offense, neither to the Jews, nor to the Greeks [Gentiles], nor to the church of God" (v. 32).

Three Lines

The verse segregates humanity into three classes: Jew, Gentile, and the church of God. As we study the Scriptures, we find that all Scripture is segmented along these lines. Consequently, it would be possible to draw three literal lines on a chart and compile portions of Scripture in relationship to what they say about these three distinguishable elements. As we shall discover, God has a program for the Jewish people. It is distinct from His plan for the church. Therefore, when the program for Israel is confused with the program for the church, much of Scripture, and history for that matter, becomes unintelligible. It is abundantly clear from such passages as Romans 11:1 that God has not cast away His people—Israel has a national and a historical future.

Thankfully, He also describes the course and destiny of a Gentile world system that is hostile to God and His people. It is comforting to learn that there will be a payday someday for a world system that glories in shaking its fist in the face of God and His Christ. Of course, in the process of destroying Gentile belligerence, the Lord also deals with the premier perpetrators of evil, human or demonic—the Antichrist and his mentor and empowerer, Satan.

On the third line, positioned between those of the Jews and the Gentiles, is the church, which is not an extension of Judaism nor a part of Gentilism. The church is a totally unique entity called into being by God for a specific purpose and given only a specific period of time to work on earth. His church is on a mission, moved forward by an obsession. When it is "mission completed" for the church, we are destined to be Raptured out of this world.

No Middle Wall

Ephesians 2 and 3 is a pinnacle portion of the Word of God regarding teaching about the church. The new relationship between believing Jews and believing Gentiles is a central theme of the passage and clarifies the composition of the body of Christ.

Gentiles are described as those who are by nature the children of wrath, even as others. They are without God, aliens from the commonwealth of Israel, estranged from the covenants and having no hope in this world. In short, the Gentile condition is aptly described as being dead in trespasses and sins—that is, until the Messiah, our Lord Jesus, stepped in with His unspeakable gift.

> *For by grace are ye saved through faith; and that not of yourselves, it is the gift of God—Not of works, lest any man should boast. For we are his workmanship, created in Christ Jesus unto good works, which God hath before ordained that we should walk in them* (Ephesians 2:8-10).

How was it all accomplished?

By His cross.

Here He brought together the most monumental of truths, using the imagery of the Old Testament Temple that stood on Mount Moriah in Jerusalem. Speaking of Gentiles, He said, "But now in Christ Jesus ye who once were far off are made near by the blood of Christ. For he is our peace, who hath made both one, and hath broken down the middle wall of partition between us" (Ephesians 2:13-14).

The old fence that stood between the Court of the Gentiles and the courts frequented by Jewish worshipers kept Gentiles at a distance. There was no access to the sacred altar, the Israelite court, or the Temple itself. Gentiles were denied access. Through the cross work of Christ, that partition, symbolic of separation, was broken down. And the animosity between Jews and Gentiles was swept away with its debris.

We can all remember when the Berlin Wall was torn down and long-separated people were reunited in the aftermath of its destruction. Few will forget the euphoria of the time and the satisfaction of knowing that the divider had come down. Especially vivid were the scenes of East and West Germans, many of them relatives, embracing as they were reunited. This historic event, in a beggarly sort of way, pictures what occurred when the wall that kept Jews and Gentiles apart came down.

Twin Remnants

When the middle wall of partition was broken down, it was time to join the remnants, for now there was peace between those who were formerly estranged. The enmity was no more. It is a vast understatement to say that this was a new thing. God treats it as a major, divinely driven event, one that would change the course of future relationships on this planet.

Believing Jews and believing Gentiles were hereafter to comprise "one new man...one body by the cross" (Ephesians 2:15-16) and become "fellow citizens with the saints, and of the household of God" (Ephesians 2:19), built together "upon the foundation of the apostles and prophets, Jesus Christ himself being the chief corner stone" (Ephesians 2:20).

With this great wonder of wonders fully in view, there was something else. God was, in His church, beginning to construct a sanctuary. *"In whom [Jesus Christ] all the building fitly framed together groweth unto an holy temple in the Lord; In whom ye also are built together for an habitation of God through the Spirit"* (Ephesians 2:21-22).

If you remember the instruction Jesus gave to His disciples in John about the ministry of the Holy Spirit in the new age of grace, you will recall that He said that the Holy Spirit would not only abide with them, but He "shall be in you." In Ephesians 2 we begin to experience the fullness of His word to them.

This is no better illustrated than in the sense of family experienced by Jewish and Gentile believers today. A few months ago, some friends and I were invited to a Passover Seder service at the home of a colleague in Jerusalem. When we arrived at his home, we found more than 50 people who had come to share the joy of the evening. There were Europeans, Americans, Russians, and Israelis—Jews and Gentiles—crammed into the limited space our host's home provided. We heard the story of the Passover—the same story told in every Jewish home celebrating the event the world over.

Following a sumptuous meal, our host stood to tell the rest of the story. It was centered around how *"Christ, our passover, is sacrificed for us"* (1 Corinthians 5:7). There we sat in Jerusalem, two thousand years after Jesus had done the same thing with His little band of disciples in the upper room. Although many of us did not speak the same language, we were joined in one spirit as family in Christ. The middle wall has indeed been broken down, and two millennia later we represent elements of the living sanctuary He promised to build.

His Wisdom, His Glory

The Ephesian portrait goes on to make two captivating points.

"To the intent that now, unto the principalities and powers in heavenly places, might be known by the church the manifold wisdom of God" (Ephesians 3:10).

So unique is the church that God has chosen to put it on display before principalities and powers in other realms. Simply put, He has invited humans, the angelic host, friend and foe, and all who care to look, to come and behold what only God could do: make believing Jews and believing Gentiles "fellow heirs, and of the same body, and partakers of his promise in Christ by the gospel" (Ephesians 3:6).

This He calls "the manifold wisdom of God."

There can be no mistake about it: The greatest testimony of the power of the gospel is when believing Jewish people sit down with believing Gentiles as a family in Christ. It is the grand contradiction of every stereotype the world has to offer. Only the gospel can produce this glorious manifestation.

It is so glorious that before closing His word on the subject in Ephesians 3, we find this marvelous benediction:

"Unto him be glory in the church by Christ Jesus throughout all ages, world without end. Amen" (Ephesians 3:21).

So then, the church is depicted as not only the very wisdom of God, but the manifestation of His glory as well. All of this emanates from Christ through His redeemed twin remnants.

Undeniably the church is made up of a special people who are sent on a particular mission—one not envisioned by the prophets of the Old Testament. But ours is a mission that embodies the very essence of what God is accomplishing during this age of grace.

Don't Forget Israel

Does the presence of the church mean that God is through with Israel and now, as some teach, the church has become spiritual Israel? Far from it. The question is eloquently answered by the Apostle Paul in Romans 11:1: *"I say, then, Hath God cast away his people? God forbid. For I also am an Israelite, of the seed of Abraham, of the tribe of Benjamin."*

While Paul emphatically declared that the Jewish remnant is a fact of life in this church age—*"Even so, then,"* he asserted, *"at this present time also there is a remnant according to the election of grace"* (Romans 11:5)—he was as certain that there is coming a day when God will again deal with the nation of Israel.

We will return to Israel's place in God's program later because it is, of course, a fundamental proposition in the biblical scheme of things. Related to this is the fact that much false teaching has arisen because the divine plans for Israel and the church have been mixed or confused.

Payday's Coming

The final revelation on the divine prophetic time line follows the course and destiny of a Gentile world—a world system that is headed for a collision with catastrophe. We will expand on this theme in chapter 7. Suffice it to say at this point that the destruction of Gentile world power will be thorough. Daniel 2, speaking collectively of the great empires that will come to the scene across the centuries, gives us a dramatic foreview.

> And in the days of these kings shall the God of heaven set up a kingdom, which shall never be destroyed; and the kingdom shall not be left to other people, but it shall break in pieces and consume all these kingdoms, and it shall stand forever. Forasmuch as thou sawest that the stone was cut out of the mountain without hands, and that it broke in pieces the iron, the bronze, the clay, the silver, and the gold, the great God hath made known to the king what shall come to pass hereafter; and the dream is certain, and the interpretation of it sure (Daniel 2:44-45).

A Footnote

I never feel more in touch with what we have discovered in Ephesians than when I am at Jerusalem's memorial to the Holocaust, Yad Vashem, with my friend Zvi. It is a place where the emblems of suffering and death are everywhere in evidence. If there is a doubt in anyone's mind about the historical reality of the grim days suffered by Jews in Hitler's Europe, they need but spend a few hours at Yad Vashem. In a way, it is a singular manifestation of

Satan's attempt, through demonically driven Gentile human agents, to exterminate the Chosen People.

To walk there with Zvi, a Jewish survivor of the Holocaust, magnifies the triumph of the cross over the worst that mankind can do. Zvi, a Jew, and I, a Gentile, walk together among the terrible relics of that tragic time. But we are not there as avowed enemies. We are there as brothers in the Lord, sharing the family relationship that is normal for believers in Jesus— normal only because that middle wall of partition has been forever broken down.

The simple fact is that Paul did not know when Christ would return. He was in the exact position in which we are. All that he knew, and all that we know, is that Christ may come at any moment.

—R. C. H. Lenski

Chapter Three

ONE HOPE,
ONE MISSION

Many people who are now believers were strongly
motivated to trust Christ as Savior because of the
conviction that the Lord might come and find them unprepared.
This was certainly true in my own experience. I was not reared in
a Christian home and seldom attended church services. When I
did, it was at a local church where the message of Christ had given
way to the social gospel. My first exposure to a true gospel message was at the Colosseum in Detroit, Michigan. A Hebrew-
Christian evangelist, Dr. Hyman Appleman, brought a message on
the Second Coming of Christ.

When I left the building that evening, although still unsaved, I firmly believed three things:

- First, the Bible was the Word of God.
- Second, Jesus was coming again.
- Third, should He appear, I was not ready to meet Him.

From that day until the day when I trusted Christ as my personal Savior, I was driven by two increasingly overwhelming concerns. *What if I should die before I became a Christian? What if He should come in the night and find me unprepared?*

I can remember thunderstorms, the kind we had in Michigan, with the black clouds seeming to swirl just above the housetops. During those dark, rain-spattered days, with bright lightning flashes and thunderclaps drumming the sky, it was as though, in my mind's eye, I could see Jesus just beyond the clouds, ready to break through and find me lost. That seems like a long time ago. It was, and the acute fear of being found wanting is now lost in the assurance of being ready to meet Him. But there is a point to be made. What I experienced as an unsaved young man was totally compatible with what the Scripture clearly teaches about the imminent return of Jesus Christ for His church.

His imminent return simply means that Christ may come at any moment. There is nothing that must transpire—no sign manifestations—before He comes to call His own home, as He promised in John 14.

The Two Dimensions of the Mission of the Church

Remember what we have learned about the church. It is unique in its composition and mission. Israel has its signs of the last days that serve as warnings of the nearness of His great second advent coming. No signs are promised for the church, however. But although no signs are promised, two things are required.

To Make Him Known

Before Jesus ascended into heaven from the Mount of Olives, He issued a command to His disciples. The kingdom was to be postponed, He told them, but they were being sent on a mission—one that was to be their consuming passion until He came for them.

"But ye shall receive power, after the Holy Spirit is come upon you; and ye shall be witnesses unto me both in Jerusalem, and in all Judœa, and in Samaria, and unto the uttermost part of the earth" (Acts 1:8).

The mission of the church, simply stated, is to make Him known. In this day when much of evangelical Christianity is moving into an era of horizontal rather than vertical ministry postures, we need a revival of that commitment to evangelism. When I refer to a horizontal mindset, I am referring to the current passion for personal relationships. Doctrine and even confessions of faith are minimized or ignored in favor of warm—we might even say *huggy*—relationships with fellow humans. The vertical view promotes relationships based on an up-front, loving presentation of the gospel message—making Him known. That, after all, is what we have been called to do. Exhibiting civility toward others, whoever they may be, is, of course, part and parcel of Christian conduct. It is not, however, the end that we seek. It is but a means to share the genuineness of our faith.

Many people are disturbed to realize that evangelistic campaigns are virtually nonexistent in many of our churches. They seem to have gone the way of the hymnal as we adopt more contemporary worship forms. But although things may be done in many different ways as society changes, we must remember that the commission remains unaltered: We must make Him known.

A wonderful old missionary song catches the essence of what we are called to do in a wonderful way.

> Give of thy sons to bear the message glorious;
> Give of thy wealth to speed them on their way.

My wife Maxine and I have had the heartwarming experience of seeing this transacted within our own family. After years of a successful business career, our son, Andy, and his wife Gwen felt a call to the mission field. Today they are joyfully making Christ known in the land of Paraguay. We feel that it is a great privilege to stand by them as they labor to bring the gospel to others.

Our experience is, of course, not unique or superior to that of millions of earnest believers across the centuries who have been happy to give of their sons and daughters to take the torch of truth to benighted people in distant places.

But whether we are called to go or commissioned to stay put, the charge is as intense: Make Him known! Make Him known! Make Him known!

When we study the Book of Acts, what do we find? As the apostles and their companions went on successive missionary journeys, they purposed in city after city to proclaim Christ to Jews and Gentiles alike. As churches were formed, they developed ministries to meet the spiritual and physical needs of the people. These subsidiary functions became necessary only because the name of Christ was preached, hearts were convicted of sin, and men and women came to know Him.

This is one reason why I believe that God has sheltered the church from the obligation to look for signs. I'm sure you have noticed that when some people become enamored with looking for signs of the end times, they tend to become obsessed with the subject—so much so that they forget what they are here to do. Primarily, we are here to proclaim the gospel and develop support ministries that will nurture and serve believers.

The Date-Guessing Game

Setting dates for the Rapture of the church seems to be turning into a cottage industry these days. I remember a man out West a few years ago who had worked out a series of calculations that, in his scheme of things, proved that the Rapture would occur on a given day. His plan was so detailed that he had charts for every time zone with information as to the time the event would occur at any given place on earth. As is often done in such cases, people sold properties in preparation for the great day. Needless to say, the man to whom this momentous revelation had been given was, temporarily, a sought-after celebrity. He was often seen on TV, quoted in newspapers, and heard on radio interview shows—that is, until the day came, and passed, and the Lord did not put in an appearance.

When the Lord failed to come, the man was promptly and properly discredited, while his followers scrambled to recover their goods and restore their reputations.

I do not say this to open old wounds or to further embarrass people whom we should be attempting to turn to more sound biblical teaching. I do say it to remind us all that the Lord consistently warns us to stay away from the folly of date setting, and for a very good reason.

The Rapture of the church has nothing to do with a date. I repeat: It has nothing to do with a date. Once we learn this, we will never again be tempted to sate our curiosity by reading or hearing details of some novel new approach to the Rapture question.

There is a word in Scripture that makes a very clear point on this matter. Romans 11, which speaks of the future program for Israel yet to be fulfilled, says this about the church: *"For I would not, brethren, that ye should be ignorant of this mystery, lest ye should be wise in your own conceits: that blindness in part is happened to Israel, until the fullness of the Gentiles be come in"* (v. 25).

When Paul referred to "the fullness of the Gentiles," he was not speaking of "the times of the Gentiles" mentioned by Jesus in the Gospels. He was specifically referring to the completion of the gathering of the bride of Christ (the church). It is important to note what he went on to say in verse 26.

"And so," he said, *"all Israel shall be saved; as it is written, There shall come out of Zion the Deliverer, and shall turn away ungodliness from Jacob."*

There is an obvious break between verses 25 and 26. In verse 25 Paul was speaking of the conclusion of the church age—"the fullness of the Gentiles be come in"—before moving on to a discussion of the time when God will begin to reinstitute His program for Israel's national reconciliation to the Messiah (v. 26).

The fullness of the Gentiles is not related to the appearing of certain signs or debatable elements. Rather, it implies the completion of a program designed to gather a given number of Gentiles. We can therefore safely assume that the Rapture—which will occur just before "the time of Jacob's trouble [Israel's Tribulation]" (Jeremiah 30:7)—is associated more with a number than with a date. It is a number that is obviously known only to God. It is not hidden amidst the signs of Scripture, nor is it inscribed in some obscure region of biblical numerology. No. When the church has been gathered—the last of the redeemed brought in—the church will be caught away, as He promised.

All of this demonstrates the futility of setting dates and guarantees that date setters will continue to be one hundred percent wrong in their predictions. Furthermore, it brings a fresh challenge to the church to redouble its efforts in evangelism, the first priority.

To Look for Him

The First Epistle to the Thessalonians is a book saturated with expectancy and longing for the Rapture of the church. A standard is set in the first chapter, where the Apostle Paul was commenting on the Thessalonians' conversion from paganism and their subsequent lifestyle as Christian believers. So exemplary was their conduct as Christians that they became "an example to all that believe in Macedonia" (1 Thessalonians 1:7).

> For they themselves show of us what man-
> ner of entering in we had unto you, and how
> ye turned to God from idols, to serve the liv-
> ing and true God, *And to wait for his Son from
> heaven, whom he raised from the dead, even
> Jesus, who delivered us from the wrath to
> come* (1 Thessalonians 1:9-10).

Their lives were marked by twin evidences of the reality of their faith and the quality of their love for the Savior.
First, they were reaching out to other lost men and women
around them. "For from you sounded out the word of the
Lord not only in Macedonia and Achaia, but also in every
place your faith toward God is spread abroad" (1
Thessalonians 1:8).

While their hand was to the plow, so to speak, their eyes were
fixed on the heavens as they waited eagerly for the coming of
the Savior. These Thessalonian Christians were not looking to
some dim, distant, after-the-trial-by fire scenario as the hope of
their deliverance. No indeed. They were already enduring
severe affliction. But in its midst, they lived with a daily expectation: Perhaps today! That was the theme of their lives.
Maranatha was the very watchword of their existence.

So taken were they with the imminent return of Christ that
they evidently believed that He would come for them before
any of them died. In the famous Rapture passage found in the
fourth chapter, Paul spoke to their concerns about "them who
are asleep" (v. 13).

The Thessalonians were resting in the fact that they were
"delivered from the wrath to come"—the Tribulation period.
But they were confused about the saints who were taken in
death before the Rapture.

This imminent return of Christ for His own is properly called the "blessed hope."

> Teaching us that, denying ungodliness and worldly lusts, we should live soberly, righteously, and godly, in this present age, *Looking for that blessed hope, and the glorious appearing of the great God and our Savior, Jesus Christ,* Who gave himself for us that he might redeem us from all iniquity, and purify unto himself a people of his own, zealous of good works" (Titus 2:12-14).

This central passage about the "blessed hope" puts the best of what Christianity is about into perfect focus. It evokes a life of intimate association with our Lord that produces a godly life, one that gives moment-by-moment evidence of the desire to see Him face to face. It is, furthermore, a life charged with zeal for the Lord, the proclamation of the gospel, and service for Him through good works.

Incidentally, these attributes put to rest the oft-raised straw-man idea that if people are looking for the imminent return of Christ, they will be tempted to become slovenly Christians. Actually, just the opposite is true. Those who love His appearing and expect Him momentarily are much more apt to keep their house in order than those who think He is delaying His coming.

Watching and Waiting

So, here it is, God's program for His called-out people: Make Him known; keep looking for Him.

Have you ever noticed the number of gospel songs and hymns that are devoted to the Rapture theme? This is true, I'm sure, because it is the ultimate expression of the believer's hope. There is a buoyancy—a joy—a refreshing feeling that what we experience when we come together as a worshiping family may consummate, at that very moment, in our moving over into glory. Let's sample a phrase from a hymn that says it well.

Watching and waiting, looking above,
Filled with His goodness, lost in His love.

There is a wellspring of purity and simplicity in the mission and hope He has given to us. Think about it. Although there are many responsibilities attached to being a responsible Christian, we have but one overriding commission: to make Him known. It is something every believer, in his or her own way, is perfectly capable of doing. One of the most effective soul winners I have ever known was a man who was illiterate. But the radiance of his witness and the simple dedication of his life drew others to Christ like a magnet.

We are called to a singular purpose, and it is the purest of objectives: peopling heaven!

And we are to be looking for Him—like children standing by the door in the evening waiting for a loving father to arrive home. There is a fusion of purity and simplicity found here that is hard to duplicate. Children waiting for the sound of His voice—"Watching and waiting, looking above." I guess that says it pretty well.

Nowhere is a date set, nor was there any definite promise that the consummation would occur within the lifetime of the first-century Christians. Nevertheless, the possibility of the Lord's advent was always present.

—Merrill C. Tenney

Chapter Four

IF I SHOULD
DIE...

"25 Killed in Jerusalem, Ashkelon Attacks."

S o read the headline in today's *Jerusalem Post.* The story goes on to tell of 84 more people who were wounded in the horrible suicide attacks carried out by Muslim fanatics. Hamas agents detonated the devices just a few blocks from where I sit as I write this morning. At this moment, like a reminder of yesterday's horror, I can hear the wail of an ambulance siren coming up to my window from far down on the street.

It is not enough to say that such indiscriminate acts of terror are a tragedy. Those forced to view the carnage wreaked in the bombed-out buses have a memory etched on their minds that will never be erased. I am looking at it now, in a photograph of the faces of three young girls lamenting the death of a young friend who was unfortunate enough to be caught too near one of the bombs. The faces say all that there is to be said: Someone has been killed. Theirs is the summary expression worn by the grief stricken the world over. It is the look of the foremost perplexity faced by our kind.

"Why must we die?"

Yes, without question, the most heartrending of all perplexities faced by human beings is the dilemma of death. Any number of examples have crossed the pages of the biblical record. The Shunammite, who fell at the feet of Elisha in the throes of sorrow over the death of her young son, demonstrates clearly not only the power of the sting of death but God's tender care for those who have fallen victim to the grim reaper.

You will remember little Martha and Mary who lived at Bethany with their brother Lazarus. So devastated were they with grief and despair at his untimely passing that both sisters mildly rebuked the Lord when He arrived—as they saw things—late for the funeral.

"If thou hadst been here," said aggrieved Martha, "my brother had not died" (John 11:21). Mary echoed the same rejoinder when she came into the presence of the Lord a bit later.

"If thou hadst been here!"

That phrase catches extremely well, I think, the emotion that most frequently grips the hearts of those who have felt the barbs of death's arrows. "Where was God when I needed Him most?" We've all seen it in the faces of family members, friends, and loved ones who have been forced to leave behind the folded physical tent of one dear to them.

I suppose we could have seen it in the face of the widow of Nain as she followed the bier containing the remains of her dear son out of her little town. It most certainly would have been reflected in the visage of the ruler of the Capernaum synagogue, Jairus, when the awful fact of his daughter's death sank into the depths of his soul.

I, along with an almost endless procession of ministers, have seen it and shared the impotent sensation of someone expected to say just the right thing when he knew that he could not.

You see, death is so foreign to everything we hold dear in life that when forced to face it, there are few who are up to the moment. It is a time when only two sources can accomplish what we cannot. First, there is the assurance from the Lord that He will never leave those who trust Him as Savior and Lord. "I will," He said, "never leave thee, nor forsake thee" (Hebrews 13:5). Thus, according to His promise, the Holy Spirit will be the source of comfort, ministering to us in ways that we are not capable of doing. For this reason, a Christian should not be intimidated or humiliated when he or she finds less than adequate words of comfort for grieving brothers or sisters in the faith. We must remind ourselves that God is competent and can, in ways known only to Himself, speak the comfort needed at such times.

Then there is the promise of the Word. It is only there that people find the correct information regarding the whereabouts of their loved ones taken in death.

Like a Grain of Wheat

Our Lord must have a very special place in His heart for those who are smitten by the perplexity of death—He has taken so much care to answer our questions in the Scriptures. The Word first gives us a general and observable illustration of life and death. We see it all about us. Speaking of His own death and resurrection, Jesus said, *"Except a grain of wheat fall into the ground and die, it abideth alone; but if it die, it bringeth forth much fruit"* (John 12:24). He was speaking primarily of His own death and the eternal benefits that are reaped by believers through His sacrifice. The wheat must wither and die, but in that very withering is the promise of new life and abundance.

The same is said of us in 1 Corinthians 15:42-44. *"So also is the resurrection of the dead. It is sown in corruption; it is raised in incorruption. It is sown in dishonor; it is raised in glory. It is sown in weakness; it is raised in power. It is sown a natural body; it is raised a spiritual body."* These bodies in which we walk about are described as bare grain, just a kind of seed. Their withering and dying are as natural as life itself—and not only natural, but necessary.

It is before us, in a general way, in the seasons as they come and go. For most of us, the onset of fall brings on a mild sense of melancholy. Something is beginning to pass from among us. The balm of summer is slipping away.

The worst is yet to come. And it does. Winter winds and dreadful February are inevitable. But with March comes the earth's stirring, and we find ourselves in much better spirits. By Easter's dawn, and with the robe of spring fully upon us, the bare grain has become the flower promised at the falling of the first leaf of the old season.

So it is with life and death. But, as natural revelation gives irrefutable evidence of the existence of God, much more specific detail must be found in order to obtain salvation. In much the same way, the witness of the seasons awakens us to the fact that more must be learned about this grim business of life and death and how we are to go on from here.

If I Should Die...

The old spirituals sang of it with acute expectation.

"Soon I will be done with the troubles of the world—Goin' home to live with God!" And what a homegoing it was to be: clothed in golden slippers and shimmering apparel, far beyond the lash of wearisome trials and tribulations. "Goin' home to live with God!"

Some of the longing and wonder expressed in those simple phrases are lost to most of us now—until. Until, that is, death steps in, the universally unwanted visitor. It comes to strike us with such ferocity that, whether we know the words or not, the questions and hopes raised in those old spirituals are awakened within us once again.

As a child, I knew one prayer: "If I should die before I wake, I pray the Lord my soul to take." I prayed that prayer

often as a youngster, mostly late at night, with its strange
sounds and ghostly images pressing in on me. In those
days I did not have the slightest notion what actually happened when a person died. It was all shrouded in a very
unsettling sort of darkness.

Paul had no such difficulty, and we find in his words, com-
municated to us through the Holy Spirit, precise information
about what transpires when these tabernacles of clay in which
we move about are laid to rest.

> *Therefore, we are always confident, know-
> ing that, while we are at home in the body, we
> are absent from the Lord (For we walk by
> faith, not by sight); We are confident, I say,
> and willing rather to be absent from the body,
> and to be present with the Lord* (2
> Corinthians 5:6-8).

There is no sound of purgatorial purgings here, nor the
summons to call one before a works-weighted balance
scale to learn of heaven or hell. No, there is certainty
here: absent from the body, present with the Lord—an
instant transition into the arms of a waiting Savior. My
beloved mother-in-law used to say that she would be quite
content to go to sleep and wake up in heaven. Late one
night, at 88 years of age, her longing became a reality.
Mom went to bed on one shore and awakened on another.
This is the very truth—simple as it sounds—that the apostle was setting forth.

He returns to the subject in Philippians 1, where he says,

> *According to my earnest expectation and
> my hope, that in nothing I shall be ashamed,*

*but that with all boldness, as always, so now
also Christ shall be magnified in my body,
whether it be by life or by death. For to me
to live is Christ, and to die is gain...For I am
in a strait between two, having a desire to
depart and to be with Christ, which is far
better* (Philippians 1:20-23).

I'm interested in the word "boldness" found in that passage. In life or in death, we can have boldness; not necessarily aggression, but a quiet confidence in Christ's ability to bring us through.

One day I sat across the desk from Carol, who had come to my office to interview for a teaching position at our Christian day school. Her teaching credentials were impeccable; however, the moment I saw her I was convinced that she was not up to the task. Carol's body was frail and visibly misshapen. She also had a heart defect that was evident by the coloring of her skin. I was having a difficult time edging toward telling her that she would not qualify for the position. Reading my dilemma, she spoke first.

"You don't think that I am capable of doing this job, do you?"

"No," I said haltingly, "I'm afraid I do not."

"Well," Carol responded firmly, "I want you to know, Mr. McQuaid, that I am just fine, thank you." Her quiet boldness got her the job. And over the next several years Carol proved that she was right, and I was wrong.

In the end though, the strain on her inadequate heart became too much, and Carol left us. During her last hours on earth, I went to her bedside. She was unable to talk, and as I entered the room, she pointed to a small pencil and pad on the table near her bed. She wrote:

"I'm just fine, thank you."

Within hours Carol was indeed "just fine." But before leaving us, she sent a message: One can have every bit as much boldness in facing death as in facing life.

There is something very significant in the Philippian passage that is almost always overlooked when we talk of the desire to leap from the limitations of life and these bodies and bound into His presence. It is a sublime statement of attitude—a right attitude toward death, yes, but toward life as well.

Death is, we learn, after all is said and done, a sort of delivery system. It is primarily in the business of getting saints home. Some might view this as a rather strange way of looking at our old archenemy, but simply put, that is exactly what death does. However unpleasant the process may be, in the end, death serves us as a gatekeeper.

But what about our days before the great homeward call? Here's how Paul felt about it.

"Nevertheless, to abide in the flesh is more needful for you" (Philippians 1:24). *As long as you need me here, I am willing to stay.* This explains a great deal. Someone who is reading these words may be suffering from an extended, debilitating illness. Perhaps you may even be wondering if you and those around you would be better off if you were gone. God alone has the answer to that question. He alone manages the affairs of life and death for believers. So then, we can say with confidence, "Whether I understand it all or not, when I am no longer needed here

and He has better things for me to do on the other side, then I'll cross over."

To Know as We are Known

Will we know our loved ones on the other side? This question is often asked. The short answer is, of course, yes. We will know our loved ones.

On the Mount of Transfiguration, millennia before their bodies were scheduled for resurrection, Moses and Elijah were recognized by Peter, James, and John (see Matthew 17:1-8; Mark 9:2-13; Luke 9:28-36).

When David's child was taken in the aftermath of his consorting with Bathsheba, he did something that others thought was very strange. While the baby lay dying, he refused to be consoled. When the child died, he rose up, washed, worshiped, and called for food. His servants wanted to know why.

> While the child was yet alive, I fasted and wept; for I said, Who can tell whether GOD will be gracious to me, that the child may live? But now he is dead, why should I fast? Can I bring him back again? *I shall go to him, but he shall not return to me* (2 Samuel 12:22-23).

David was certain of two things: The child was safe in God's keeping. He also knew that the child had been created as a totally unique being and that his identity would be retained until the day they met again.

Look about you. There are 5 billion people on this planet. Other than identical twins, how many of them look

alike? This fact alone confirms God's purpose in retaining
personal identities. Is He less careful for His arrangement
here than He will be there? I think we all know the answer
to that question.

How Will We be Clothed?

My granddaughter asks a similar question with every
sunrise. "Mother, what will I wear today?" A follow-up
query is often, "Are we going to the mall today?" At two
years of age, she has a very keen sense of appearance.
Correct me if I'm wrong, but I believe this is something
that is God-induced. You will recall that Adam and Eve
were extremely concerned about their attire, or lack of it,
in the Garden of Eden (see Genesis 3:7-10).

Our heavenly bodies are described as "spiritual": "As we
have borne the image of the earthy, we shall also bear the
image of the heavenly" (1 Corinthians 15:49).

Temporarily being robed with garments made white by
His blood is but preparation for the day of our *coming out*
in heavenly vestments designed for each of us according to
His specifications.

> *For our citizenship is in heaven, from
> which also we look for the Savior, the Lord
> Jesus Christ, Who shall change our lowly
> body, that it may be fashioned like his glori-
> ous body, according to the working by which
> he is able even to subdue all things unto him-
> self* (Philippians 3:20-21).

A body and garments of glory like His very own? What is it that the songwriter said?

> But lo! There breaks a yet more glorious day;
> The saints triumphant rise in bright array;
> The King of Glory passes on His way.
> Alleluia! Alleluia!

That's good, very good; but it doesn't even come close.

There will be many things happening in heaven if we should be called home before the Rapture. We are given a few glimpses here and there, but hardly the entire picture. We are permitted to look in on the heavenly scene in Revelation and see that there is worship.

> The four and twenty elders fall down before him that is seated on the throne, and worship him that liveth forever and ever, and cast their crowns before the throne, saying, Thou art worthy, O Lord, to receive glory and honor and power; for thou hast created all things, and for thy pleasure they are and were created (Revelation 4:10-11).

There's a new song being sung, but it has a very old theme.

> And they sang a new song, saying, Thou art worthy...for thou wast slain, and hast redeemed us to God by thy blood out of every kindred, and tongue, and people, and nation" (Revelation 5:9).

It reminds me of the gospel song, "There's Power in the Blood," that we once heard heartily sung in our churches.

There is also a reminder of service for Christ, for in Revelation 5:10 the redeemed are looking ahead to reigning with Him: "And hast made us unto our God a kingdom of priests, and we shall reign on the earth" (Revelation 5:10).

The capstone, I think, is placed in two wonderful verses. John says,

> And I beheld, and I heard the voice of many angels round about the throne and the living creatures and the elders, and the number of them was ten thousand times ten thousand, and thousands of thousands, Saying with a loud voice, Worthy is the Lamb that was slain to receive power, and riches, and wisdom, and strength, and honor, and glory, and blessing" (Revelation 5:11-12).

Taking notice of the information given to us, several things become clear. When we are ushered into His presence, yes, we will be in the midst of heretofore unseen beauty and things that can only pertain to heaven. However, there is also the ring of familiarity about the entire experience.

- Worshiping
- Singing
- Serving

All of these things are familiar to us in the here and now. Thus, when our loved ones—whether children or elderly saints—"go home to glory," they are, in point of fact, going home. They are not entering a strange, new reality.

In addition to this, as well as being with Him, we will enter a circle of familiar faces, those in that "so great a cloud of witnesses" (Hebrews 12:1) that has preceded us. Today there are, in our little life circles, missing faces. They are not here. They are with our Lord in the place He has so carefully prepared. The only thing that will change when we leave this earth will be the circle of faces surrounding us. Those still toiling here will be temporarily out of view.

And so we find that we can be comforted as the ones we love pass from us. It is only temporary; they are safe and well, covered with the riches of a love that we cannot supply. Allow me to say it once again: They are at home.

A man whose wife had preceded him to glory was being consoled by a friend.

"I am sorry about the loss of your wife," he said. "It must have been very difficult for you."

"Oh, but she is not lost," the man replied. "I know exactly where she is and just where she will be when I arrive."

Looking for that blessed hope, and the glorious appearing of the great God and our Savior, Jesus Christ.

—Paul

Chapter Five

THREE COMFORTS

We were visiting the Mount Herzl Cemetery in Jerusalem. The place is to Israel what Arlington National Cemetery is to the United States. The names of such Israeli leaders as Theodor Herzl, Golda Meir, and the late Prime Minister Levi Eshkol are etched in Hebrew on the large blocks of black granite covering the grave sites.

We had come to visit the grave of Yitzhak Rabin, who had been so tragically struck down a few months before. Interspersed among the columns of soldiers and small groups of civilians who came to pay their respects were several groups of young children, each child carrying a small memorial candle to be lit and placed on the grave.

As I walked along the way where the graves of other digni-
taries are located, my wife waited on a bench beside a middle-
aged blond woman.

"You should have been here a few moments ago, when that
group of children were here," the woman remarked.

"They stood around the grave, many of them weeping soft-
ly, as one of them recited a prayer for the dead. It was very
moving."

Maxine responded by saying how touched she is each time
she visits Yad Vashem, especially the memorial for the one and
a half million Jewish children who perished in the Holocaust.

The woman confided that she felt the same emotions, but for
slightly different reasons.

"You see," she explained, "I am a German journalist. As a
journalist, I am supposed to be able to control my emotions.
But when I think of what was done to these people in my country, I am so troubled...." Her voice trailed off as she broke
down and began to weep.

Troubling indeed, but much more so when you wonder just
how many of the estimated 50 million who died in Hitler's
monstrous war of aggression died without hope.

Three Comforts

We know that there were countless thousands among them
who did have hope—an eternal hope. For them, to be absent
from the body was to be present with the Lord (see 2
Corinthians 5:8). Beyond that, there was the hope of the any-
moment return of Christ to call them home in the Rapture.
How many, I wonder, engulfed in the flames of battle, cried for

the coming of the Lord. Their hope was not a vain expression born of some fanatical aspect of an equally vain religion. It is the bedrock of biblical reality.

The most impressive of all passages on the Rapture question is certainly 1 Thessalonians 4. Those marvelous verses, however, are surrounded by calls to be comforted.

Comforted in Their Faith

Paul's concern for the believers in Thessalonica, who were under intense suffering, prompted him to send *"Timothy, our brother and minister of God, and our fellow worker in the gospel of Christ, to establish you, and to comfort you concerning your faith"* (1 Thessalonians 3:2).

Timothy was dispatched to comfort those people who were in severe trial by reminding them of the quality of their faith in Christ and the promises of the Scriptures to bring them through such times of anguish. He reminded them that, indeed, difficult times would be their lot, but they should not be discouraged. Rather, they should be comforted by the fact that their afflictions were actually a source of strength that gave evidence of the reality of their faith.

The apostle was overjoyed to learn of their steadfast "faith and love" (3:6) and was thus himself comforted in the fact that they were overcomers.

At the present time, many thousands of our brethren are undergoing intense suffering for their faith in Christ. It has been said, and I believe it is true, that more Christians have been martyred for their faith in our lifetime than in the entire history of the church. Looking back on the millions killed by the communists in the former Soviet Union and China tends to confirm the assertion.

In places like Sudan and Lebanon, believers today are being driven from their homes, starved, and murdered. Sudanese children have been separated from their families and sold into slavery by Islamic extremists. Egyptian Christians have, for the last few years, found themselves susceptible to being suddenly shot down in the streets by enemies of the government and of their faith in Christ.

For decades, Liberia, in West Africa, was a model of order and stability. Christianity flourished in the country colonized by former slaves from America. Among my fondest memories of pastoral days is viewing missionary slide presentations depicting the smiling faces of eager Liberian believers worshiping the Lord they had come to love. Now the missionary families who had such a heart-love for the Liberian people are gone. The streets of the cities and towns are filled with roaming, armed bands of thugs, killing suspected rivals at will. We can only wonder how many of those smiling Christians have been victims of the terror.

What do believers in such circumstances have to cling to that will bring them through their darkest hours? It is the same reality of relationship that has brought believers through the flames of suffering and hardship for nearly two thousand years—faith in the risen Christ and in the comfort of the faith ministered by the Holy Spirit.

Paul continued his words regarding their comfort in the faith by saying, *"For now we live, if ye stand fast in the Lord. For what thanks can we render to God again for you, for all the joy with which we joy for your sakes before our God"* (1 Thessalonians 3:8-9).

The idea seems to be that Paul and his companions were now *really living* when they heard of the consistency of their beleaguered brethren in Thessalonica. They were greatly comforted and encouraged by the power of the gospel evidenced in these believers.

Comforted by the Reality of the Rapture

Their second comfort comes in chapter 4, verse 18, and relates directly to the Rapture. Their questions were: What has become of our loved ones who have died? Where are they? What will become of them in the future?

Paul reassured them with a detailed explanation bursting with comfort and profound in its simplicity. Thus he could conclude, *"Wherefore, comfort one another with these words."* In fact, Christians have been doing just that for nearly two millennia.

In the next chapter we will walk slowly through the portion of the Word devoted to the subject of the Rapture. Nowhere in Scripture do we find more riches in Christ than we do there. But first we will examine another "comfort" that is sublime in its own way.

Comforted by Escaping the Coming Tribulation

This third comfort is of immense value to believers as the darkness of the last days thickens. It is a source of comfort that should move us to a more passionate love for our Savior for His mercy and grace to us.

But of the times and the seasons, brethren, ye have no need that I write unto you. For yourselves know perfectly that the day of the Lord so cometh as a thief in the night. For when they shall say, Peace and safety, then sudden destruction cometh upon them, as travail upon a woman with child, and they shall not escape. But ye, brethren, are not in darkness, that that day should overtake you as a thief. Ye are all sons of light, and sons of the day; we are not of the night, nor of darkness. Therefore, let us not sleep, as do others, but let us watch and be sober-minded. For they that sleep sleep in the night; and they that are drunk are drunk in the night. But let us, who are of the day, be sober, putting on the breastplate of faith and love, and, for an helmet, the hope of salvation. For God hath not appointed us to wrath but to obtain salvation by our Lord Jesus Christ, Who died for us that, whether we wake or sleep, we should live together with him. Wherefore, comfort yourselves together, and edify one another, even as also ye do (1 Thessalonians 5:1-11).

In 1 Thessalonians 5:1, Paul changed the subject from the Rapture of the dead and the living who are in Christ to that of the coming time of tribulation. He spoke of tribulation of a particular kind—a kind not restricted to human belligerence or Satan's diabolical violence. The tribulation referred to here is that time of the outpouring of divine wrath on a godless world. Those who attempt, because of a particular theological bias, to squeeze the church into this chapter find themselves forced to ignore the fact that clearly the author is dealing with a subject he wished to clarify quite apart from the subject of the blessed hope.

In concluding the paragraph (5:1-11), Paul assured the saints of another "comfort." *"Wherefore,"* he said, *"comfort yourselves together, and edify one another, even as also ye do"* (5:11). It was because they had just been informed that they would have no part in the coming Tribulation. They were given a rock-solid promise. Simply stated, it is this: *"God hath not appointed us to wrath"* (5:9).

So we find three great fountainheads of comfort in 1 Thessalonians 4 and 5: comfort in our faith; comfort in our blessed hope; comfort in our deliverance from the time of Jacob's trouble.

Times and Seasons

Let's take a look at the "the times and the seasons" passage, in which Paul reminded his readers that there was really "no need that I write unto you" (5:1). Apparently he had previously instructed them on the matter of "the day of the Lord" mentioned in verse 2. His reminder came to contextualize, or put into perspective, the Rapture and the Tribulation. Believers will be present for the Rapture, absent during the coming Tribulation.

Contrasting Lifestyles

As the end of the era draws near, with its prospect of the Rapture and the Tribulation—both of which, by the way, are distinguished as coming without warning—there is a marked difference between the attitudes of believers and the people who have no heavenly hope. In a time shaded by the specter of catastrophic events, those who entertain false hopes will be saying, *"Peace and safety."* In reality, *"sudden destruction"* will be standing in the wings, ready to bring travail upon them (5:3).

We can certainly anticipate such a time by simply looking at what is happening today. The world is dotted with trouble spots, and the more talk of peace we hear, the less peace there seems to be. A distinct sign of the times can be seen in the fact that every so-called "peace agreement" brings with it a substantial number of peacekeeping troops committed to restraining those who plan to break the agreement. The thought that things will deteriorate to such an extent that the world will embrace a tyrannical Antichrist is a chilling but believable prospect. The words, "and they shall not escape" (5:3), cast an ominous warning on the inhabitants of the earth during the days of the outpouring of God's wrath. Those benighted people will live in a fantasy world—a world devoid of the light of the Word of God. While evidences of the outpouring of God's wrath mount all about them, their cry will be of "Peace and safety."

This is nothing new. Ancient Israel mirrors many instances of the same mentality. When Jerusalem was on the verge of catastrophic destruction by Babylonian invaders and the Southern tribes were embroiled in 70 years of captivity in Babylon, King Zedekiah's advisors were telling him and the nation that all was well and that there was no real threat from Babylon. "Peace and safety" was the word of the day. For his part, the Prophet Jeremiah, who was telling it like it actually was—and would be—was carted off to prison and called a trouble-maker, a plague upon the people of Israel.

The underlying motivation of the pseudo-advisors was to play on the desires of the king and the people, to tell them what they wanted to hear rather than what they desperately needed to learn. In other words, they desired, with all their hearts, peace. But to the generals of the Babylonian army, a desire for peace did not launch arrows or block the way to Jerusalem. Jewish people were feeding on false hope and were, incidentally, happy to do so. Such will be the condition of those people fed by soothing assurances from the Antichrist. They will believe that in spite of the ravages and rumblings of the early days of the Tribulation period, everything is finally under control.

Such a conclusion may very well be prompted by the exodus of the church at the Rapture. All of those "Jeremiahs" who have been sounding out warnings from God will be off the scene. For the world in general, and the newly anointed and adored Antichrist, it will be—whatever the explanation for the believers' departure—a time of great optimism. But it will be an optimism carried on the same wind of desire that mesmerized ancient Jews when the enemy was upon them.

Ancient Israel was not without a word from God, however. One of the most moving incidents in the entire episode is found in Jeremiah 37:17, when King Zedekiah commanded that Jeremiah be called from the dungeon and brought secretly into his house. In spite of what his advisors had confidently counseled, the king had an unsettling sense that all was, in fact, not well.

"Is there any word from the LORD?" he quietly asked the man with the message.

"There is," said the prophet boldly, and the news was not good. For the king and his subjects, the worst was yet to come.

So it will be with the Antichrist and his deluded followers. The "Jeremiahs" of their day will be God's two witnesses and the 144,000 Jewish believers who will be dispatched to tell it like it is—the bad news, and the better word that the King and the kingdom are coming.

First Thessalonians 5 projects the dramatic contrasts impacting the attitudes of believers who had just, in chapter 4, been instructed in the wonderful truths of the blessed hope.

"Ye, brethren, are not in darkness" (5:4), they were told.

In reality, *"Ye are all sons of light"* (5:5), they were assured.

Why? *"For God hath not appointed us to wrath but to obtain salvation by our Lord Jesus Christ"* (5:9).

These sweeping assurances lead us to the comfort and consequent edification of the release and peace of mind that comes to those with the promise of deliverance from the agonies of the Tribulation period.

As is inevitably true when we receive promises ringing with notification of grace and favor, there is also a call to responsible reaction to the riches received. In this case, it involves several things.

First, *"Therefore, let us not sleep"* (5:6).

Herein is a solemn charge to be discerners of the times and seasons; that is, to be in step with what God is doing

in these last days. It is a warning for believers to disasso-
ciate themselves from the self-indulgence and obsession
with petty non-issues that seem to be so much a part of the
evangelical scene today. I am constantly amazed at how
little many Christians seem to know or care about some of
the ominous prospects coming upon us in these last days.
We seem to be somewhat afflicted by the spirit of desire to
hope everything is OK. But things are not OK. We live in
a world awash in chaos and violence—a world needing a
clear proclamation and life-demonstration of the gospel as
never before. We are being admonished to wake up to our
obligation to be serious about our faith and seriously
engage in standing with Him in these climactic times.

Second, *"But let us, who are of the day, be sober, putting on
the breastplate of faith and love, and, for an helmet, the hope
of salvation"* (5:8).

In Ephesians 6 Paul related the breastplate to righteousness. Here he associates it with faith and love. This seems
to infer that in the waning days of the church age, there
will be a major attack on the faith that we have found in
Christ. Some of these strikes will be subtle in nature;
some, however, will be much more aggressive. One example is the escalating attack on the promise of His Second
Coming. Second Peter 3 warns that in the last days many
will say that the promise of the Rapture and Second
Coming is an empty one. Scoffers, walking after their own
lusts, are heard saying, *"Where is this coming He
promised?"* (see 2 Peter 3:4).

Not only is the promise of His coming being called into
question, but also the very identity of Christ Himself.

Palestinians, Black Muslims, Aryan Nations, Neo-Nazis, and cults of varying stripes assert that Jesus was not even a Jew, but, rather, came on the scene crafted according to their warped specifications to be used as they see fit.

Last Easter, three of the leading news magazines in the United States ran stories about the resurrection. All three contradicted the biblical and historical account of a literal resurrection. In so doing, they joined a legion of liberal theologians who had provided the inspiration for the secular magazine writers' blatant denial of the biblical facts.

Such denials are, of course, nothing new. The point is, they are becoming more numerous and intense. With serious Bible exposition at a minimum in some churches, the admonition to "put on the breastplate of faith" is timely.

"Love" is the second element accompanying the breastplate. True Christian love, manifested through godly people, is the crown of the testimony of believers. Perhaps the emphasis here is set forth as the grand contradiction to the violence and corruption so prevalent in our degenerating society. It is a matter of considerable significance that in the sequencing of Christian maturity presented in 2 Peter 1, love is the final attribute mentioned.

Faith is listed first, followed by a directive to "add to"— add virtue, knowledge, self-control, patience, godliness, brotherly kindness, and *then* love (2 Peter 1:5-7). Love is the capstone upon the "growth in grace" process through which believers are to pass. It is the evidence of a truly mature Christian. While we hear much superficial talk about love from those who choose to remain in the shallows of the Christian experience, love is actually the evi-

dence of the strength and maturity necessary to live tri-
umphantly in the last days. Thus, the love confronting us
in the Thessalonians passage is, if we may borrow a term,
the "tough love" of those willing to be tested in spiritual
combat for their faith.

Third is the "helmet, the hope of salvation" referred to in the
latter portion of 1 Thessalonians 5:8. It is a reference to the
Rapture. This becomes clear as we read the verses that follow.

"*For God hath not appointed us to wrath* but to obtain salvation
by our Lord Jesus Christ, Who died for us that, whether we wake
or sleep, we should live together with him" (5:9-10).

The great gulf standing between the "ye" and "them" designa-
tions found in this portion of Scripture is the sure hope, secured by
the one who died for us, that we will not be found among those destined for the "sudden destruction" (5:3) delivered by God in His
wrath. We are not, indeed, as the "others who have no hope"
(4:13), but are among those "not appointed...to wrath."

Is it any wonder, then, that believers are told to "comfort
yourselves together, and edify one another, even as also ye
do" (5:11)? Studying the prophetic word and rejoicing in
the doctrine of the blessed hope are things that the Apostle
Paul found commendable. They are, in fact, a great source
of comfort and strength for the church. They are also said
to be a primary source of edification for believers. This is
an effective answer to people who ridicule the study of
prophecy and those who major in confusing the issues
related to the imminent return of Christ.

No, admonished the apostle, the body of Christ is not destined
to bear His wrath—or any portion thereof. Our hope, for which
we wait expectantly, is to hear His call to come home.

And if I go and prepare a place for you, I will come again, and receive you unto myself, that where I am, there ye may be also.

—Jesus

Chapter Six

THERE IS HOPE

Believers were troubled, much as were the disciples when Jesus announced that He was going away. Members of their families were dying. Why? Had they not been expecting Him before any of them passed off the scene? This being true, why were they now forced to follow biers to freshly cut tombs to hear words, not of comfort, but of uncertainty about the future? So they wrote with haste to their surest source of information, the Apostle Paul. His answer set the landscape alight for them, and, if possible, it shines even more brilliantly upon those who await His coming today.

*But I would not have you to be ignorant,
brethren, concerning them who are asleep,
that ye sorrow not, even as others who have
no hope. For if we believe that Jesus died and
rose again, even so them also who sleep in
Jesus will God bring with him. For this we
say unto you by the word of the Lord, that we
who are alive and remain unto the coming of
the Lord shall not precede them who are
asleep. For the Lord himself shall descend
from heaven with a shout, with the voice of the
archangel, and with the trump of God; and the
dead in Christ shall rise first; Then we who
are alive and remain shall be caught up
together with them in the clouds, to meet the
Lord in the air; and so shall we ever be with
the Lord. Wherefore, comfort one another
with these words"* (1 Thessalonians 4:13-18).

Paul began his classic instruction about the Rapture of
the church with a practical preamble. The preamble was
all about how to live in an age being strangled by paganism and idolatry. His primary concern was that they
"walk...to please God" (1 Thessalonians 4:1). Their walk
to please God extended into three spheres. First was the
conduct of life in personal, moral, and spiritual matters.
Paul's concern was that their lifestyle be not "as the
Gentiles who know not God" (1 Thessalonians 4:5).
Second, he was deeply concerned about their relationships with one another: "But, as touching brotherly
love...ye yourselves are taught of God to love one another"

(1 Thessalonians 4:9). Finally, the apostle touched on their testimony toward those who were without (unbelievers): "That ye may walk honestly toward them that are outside" (1 Thessalonians 4:12).

This brief but comprehensive preparatory word answers effectively one of the primary accusations made against Christians who believe in the Rapture of the church. The argument goes something like this:

"If I believed that Christ might come at any moment, I would sit back and do nothing but wait."

Do you see the point? Belief in imminency (the any-moment return of the Lord) is said to produce a brand of believers subject to becoming so heavenly minded that they are no earthly good. It is, of course, a ludicrous argument—one designed more to discredit the doctrine of imminence than to express anything with a fiber of biblical support. In fact, virtually every passage dealing with the Rapture, such as the one before us, admonishes believers to be about the Lord's work with a great sense of urgency. Believing that the Lord is *not* coming soon is the problem—one for which there are numerous examples in the Scriptures. I cite only one.

The subject in Mark 13:32-37 is watchfulness in the light of the Lord's return. *"Watch ye, therefore,"* Jesus said, *"for ye know not when the master of the house cometh, at evening, or at midnight, or at cockcrow, or in the morning"* (v. 35). He gave the illustration of a householder to drive home the point. Like the Son, the householder took a far journey. Before leaving, he charged his servants to be watchful for his return and faithful to their duties. The specific command to the porter was "Watch!" Don't be distracted; don't be found asleep; keep on looking for the master's return.

To say the least, the sleeping servant faced dire consequences for his failure to be diligent due to the prospect of his lord's soon return.

Thus, the weight of evidence from Scripture scores heavily in favor of those who love the prospect of the Savior's return and bear life attributes that are consistent with the expectancy born of that hope.

That You Sorrow Not

"But I would not have you to be ignorant, brethren, concerning them who are asleep, that ye sorrow not, even as others who have no hope" (1 Thessalonians 4:13).

God has a marvelous way of dispelling ignorance on virtually every subject troubling the minds of believers. It is certainly the case with what He lays before us in the 1 Thessalonians 4 Rapture passage. While the world of pagan mysteries and false religions wrestles in vain to solve the problem of death and what lies beyond the grave, Christians are given instruction that banishes fear. Answers to much-debated questions come in the simplest of explanations.

Where are fellow believers who have died?

Do we face "soul sleep" after death?

Must I successfully stand at a general judgment before being permitted into His presence?

Is works/righteousness a prerequisite for heaven?

How will we meet the Lord?

As has often been stated on these pages, God gives us straight answers for the questions that are nearest our hearts' needs. The emphasis here is on rest and comfort. Troubled, sleepless nights are not a burden we are expected to bear when facing the loss of believing loved ones or our own departure from this life. We have been instructed, on the highest possible authority, that all is well. Death is, in no way, a dead end.

I sometimes wonder if we really understand just what treasures we possess in the assurances related to death and dying that we have in Christ. Perhaps the experience of a doctor who trusted Christ years ago will help to refresh our memories. He had steadfastly refused to consider the claims of Christ. Believers with whom he was acquainted had given him a clear witness to the gospel. All of this he swept away by saying that their witness was not intellectually acceptable to him. Then one day he told his friends that he had become a believer. When asked what had turned him to Christ, he replied:

"Watching Christians die!"

The difference he observed was not the alleviation of pain, but the presence of peace and certainty about the future. For the doctor, it made an eternal difference.

When the Apostle Paul used the word *asleep*, he was not referring to what is known as "soul sleep." That is the idea that when a Christian dies, body and soul are placed into a limbo-like state to await the general resurrection and march off to the judgment. The premise is made necessary because those who erroneously teach good works as essential to salvation must have a way of keeping people out of the presence of Christ until they have been judged and found worthy. But we must remember once again that our judgment took place two thousand years ago when the Lord Jesus Christ became sin for us. Furthermore, the only worthiness that we possess is that which has been granted to us by the grace of God in Christ.

For this reason, passages such as the one before us bring comfort and rest, not trepidation and outright fear. Simply stated, if we are justified on the basis of personal merit through good works, no one can ever be assured of salvation in this life.

Thus, the assurances telling us that we can know we are saved are of little value. It might be well to cite one or two examples.

"These things have I written unto you that believe on the name of the Son of God, that ye may know that ye have eternal life, and that ye may believe on the name of the Son of God" (1 John 5:13).

The proper relationship between righteousness and good works is laid out in Ephesians 2:8-10:

"For by grace are ye saved through faith; and that not of yourselves, it is the gift of God—Not of works, lest any man should boast." That's all there is to it. God purchased our redemption by the sacrifice of His Son. Then, in extreme grace, He presented it as a gift to all who will, by faith, trust Him.

Is that all there is to it? Yes—and no! Yes, that is all there is to becoming a Christian. But remember that salvation is referred to as a new birth—a beginning, not an end. What's next?

"For we are his workmanship, created in Christ Jesus unto good works, which God hath before ordained that we should walk in them" (Ephesians 2:10).

As Christians, we are committed to live a righteous life because we *are* believers—not in order to *become* believers. In short, we do what we do because we are what we are.

There is therefore no mandate to sorrow when loved ones are taken. Oh, we will miss them, to be sure. Tearful remembrances and sadness over our temporary separation are not evidences of a lack of spirituality. All the same, we rise above the wails of those who sorrow in despair of never again seeing those dearest to them.

Several years ago, I was called upon to carry out one of the tasks that seem inevitable for a father. Our second oldest son, Andy, was leaving for college in Tennessee. I was on my way to a conference in the West Indies, so we decided that I should drop him off at the school on my way to Atlanta to catch my flight. This meant that he would arrive on campus a few days before the students returned from their mid-term break.

After he was settled in at the dorm, we walked slowly toward the car. It had snowed the night before, and about four inches of the white stuff was on the ground. After we said our good-byes, I got in the car to leave. As I proceeded down the hill away from the campus, I looked in my rearview mirror. Perhaps it was a mistake.

The mirror framed my son, standing there in the snow—alone—in a strange place. I was suddenly seized by a deep sense of remorse and sorrow. I wanted him to get in the car, turn around, and go home. For the rest of my trip, I was plagued by an awful emptiness. I suppose that moment was actually good for both of us. Maybe we grew a little that day. Whether we did or not, that parting was necessary. It was right for me to feel the way I did—yes, it was necessary!

Death is a little like that—a sense of sorrow over a temporary parting. But, oh, how wonderful it will be when the morning comes.

Not so, however, for those who have no hope. A pagan is quoted to have lamented: "When the sun sets in the West, we know it will rise, come the morning. When our life is over, we go down, never to rise again."

Where Have They Gone?

Saintly singers from a generation long since gone followed the lead of Scripture when they sang,

"Steal away—! Steal away—! Steal away—to Jesus!"

Their thought was not to leave amidst an explosion of grief and anxiety. Rather, they anticipated slipping away in rest and peace as they were gently lifted by Jesus and taken into the Father's house.

Where are those who have slipped away from our presence?

"For if we believe that Jesus died and rose again, even so them also who sleep in Jesus will God bring with him" (1 Thessalonians 4:14).

Question: Where are the dead?

Answer: With Him!

You will remember, of course, the penitent thief on the cross, the one who "said unto Jesus, Lord, remember me when thou comest into thy kingdom." And Jesus replied, "Verily I say unto thee, Today shalt thou be with me in paradise" (Luke 23:42-43).

Here again we have pressed upon us the immediacy and intimacy of a right relationship with Christ. Those who know Him are literally never out of His presence. Those who "sleep in Jesus" are with Him, eagerly awaiting the coming reunion that is to take place somewhere in the clouds.

In reading the poets and philosophers so revered as the brightest lights humanity has to offer, people encounter much doom and darkness when it comes to the matter of "crossing the bar." Oh, there is the celebration of an indomitable spirit as people are confronted by the inevitable void that is death. It has the feel of empty bravado, though. That's what I thought when I was assigned to read *Invictus* as a student.

> Out of the night that covers me,
> Black as the Pit from pole to pole,
> I thank whatever gods may be
> For my unconquerable soul.
>
> In the full clutch of circumstance
> I have not winced nor cried aloud,
> Under the bludgeonings of chance
> My head is bloody, but unbowed.
>
> Beyond this place of wrath and tears
> Looms but the horror of the shade,
> And yet the menace of the years
> Finds, and shall find me, unafraid.
>
> It matters not how strait the gate,
> How charged with punishments the scroll,
> I am the master of my fate:
> I am the captain of my soul.
>   —William Ernest Henley

In reality, however, there isn't much of a choice between what their pens tell us and what the elderly pagan quoted earlier had to say. Theirs is, after all, a word of going down, never to rise again.

The difference for Christians is found in the gospel, and we are reminded of this fact at the beginning of verse 24. Assurance that the sleepers are "with him" is based on the fact that they have believed that He died and rose again. Paul reiterated the word so emphatically delivered in 1 Corinthians 15. The "gospel" he preached embodied this proposition:

"For I delivered unto you first of all that which I also received, that Christ died for our sins according to the scriptures [Isaiah 53]; And that he was buried, and that he rose again the third day according to the scriptures [Psalm 22; Isaiah 53]" (1 Corinthians 15:3-4).

The gospel assures us that we have immediate entrance into the presence of Christ and that those who have gone on to be with Him would, themselves, have us understand that all is well. For many, it has been more than simply an entrance into heaven. Rather, it has been entering into the experience longed for by the Apostle Peter when he laid bare his heart's desire for those he had nurtured in the Lord.

"For so," he told them, "an entrance shall be ministered unto you abundantly into the everlasting kingdom of our Lord and Savior, Jesus Christ" (2 Peter 1:11).

And Those Who Are Alive?

"For this we say unto you by the word of the Lord, that we who are alive and remain unto the coming of the Lord shall not precede them who are asleep" (1 Thessalonians 4:15).

Today I noticed something I had never thought much about before. (That's the way the Scriptures are—always confronting us with a fresh insight!) Note, please, that Paul said that it is "we" who are alive and remain unto His coming. Perhaps this provides a significant clue as to whether or not the apostle believed that he would personally be on the scene when the Rapture took place—I believe that he most assuredly did.

I think that there is probably a very good reason for the oversight on my part. In reading this passage, I subconsciously associate myself with the "we" who are alive and remain. And if you are among those looking for the Lord's return, I'm sure you do the same. At any rate, "we"—that is, those who are alive at His coming—will not go before the bodies of those who are with the Lord.

This word apparently was directed toward a concern that, should the Lord come and call up living saints, there would be an interval before the resurrection of the dead. Not so, said Paul. There will be no partiality in the Rapture. We will all arrive together and on time!

Here we have an explanation of the order of the Rapture. Jesus will descend into the clouds leading the company of the "dead in Christ." Their bodies will suddenly quit their graves and rise up to be glorified and reunited with the very essence of being now resting with Him in glory. Following their departure from the grave toward heaven, the living saints will be caught up to join the triumphal parade into His presence. The sense of what will transpire at the Rapture was not overdone when, years ago, singers of spirituals sang lustily of "That great gettin' up mornin'."

With Shout and Sound

"For the Lord himself shall descend from heaven with a shout, with the voice of the archangel, and with the trump of God; and

the dead in Christ shall rise first" (1 Thessalonians 4:16).

Our "great gettin' up mornin' " will be one of the most magnificent spectacles in the history of heaven.

From the cross Jesus said, *"It is finished"* (John 19:30), and it was. Redemption's work was done. His final word from the cross was a shout of victory. Now He rises to shout again. Once more, it is a shout of victory. It is His "Come forth" call for the church.

Michael the Archangel will lend his voice to the astonishing event. You will remember that Michael is the leader of the loyal angelic host standing against Satan and his consorts. His participation indicates to me that all of the created beings in the universe of God will be at attention when the saints are called home.

Following the shout will come the sounding of the trumpet. This seems to be the moment when the event will commence the grand procession into glory. Some people have proposed that the clouds mentioned in verse 17 are, in fact, clouds of angelic hosts and descending saints. Be that as it may, it will be an unprecedented event.

I think, from time to time, what it must have been like when the children of Israel made their exodus out of Egypt. I would have liked to have been there to witness that event—mile after mile of Jewish people of all ages, shapes, and descriptions in a line stretching virtually as far as the eye could see. What a sight it must have been. But it pales by comparison to what we will participate in one day soon, when it is time for the church to make its grand exodus—winding columns stretching from earth far off into the heavens.

All of which brings another such event into view. This

time, however, it will be in reverse. The record is found in Revelation 19. At the conclusion of the Tribulation period, when we will have been with Him in heaven for seven years, the heavens will open and He shall appear—not calling His own home, but bringing them with Him as He returns to the earth to reign.

"And the armies that were in heaven followed him upon white horses, clothed in fine linen, white and clean" (Revelation 19:14).

How do we know that we will be in this band? We are told specifically that when we enter His presence at the Rapture, we "shall...ever be with the Lord" (1 Thessalonians 4:17). We will never again leave His presence.

When we appear with Him at His return to earth, there will be nothing secret about it. His coming will be "as the lightning cometh out of the east, and shineth even unto the west" (Matthew 24:27).

There can be no mistake about the differences between the Rapture and the climactic Second Coming.

1. In the Rapture, the church will be taken into heaven; at the return, they will be brought to the earth.
2. The Rapture will not be preceded by signs; the return will be preceded by a plethora of signs related to Israel and the Tribulation period.
3. In the Rapture, the saints will see Him as they are drawn into His presence; at the return, "every eye shall see him, and they also who pierced him; and all kindreds of the earth shall wail because of him" (Revelation 1:7).
4. In the Rapture, only departed believers and living saints will be called to the assembly in the heavens; at His

return, the nations will be gathered for judgment.

Home At Last

"Then we who are alive and remain shall be caught up together with them in the clouds, to meet the Lord in the air; and so shall we ever be with the Lord" (1 Thessalonians 4:17).

This verse contains four facts that arouse believers to adoration and the heights of anticipation.

First, we will be caught up. First Corinthians 15:51-52 describes our coming "change."

"Behold, I show you a mystery: We shall not all sleep, but we shall all be changed, In a moment, in the twinkling of an eye, at the last trump; for the trumpet shall sound, and the dead shall be raised incorruptible, and we shall be changed."

Our being "caught up" is where we get the word *rapture*. For people who repeatedly scorn those who believe in the Rapture by saying that it is not a biblical word, there is little comfort from Scripture, because the precise meaning of the word *rapture* is the term we find in the saints being "caught up." The sensation will be better experienced than described. For the moment, it is quite enough to understand that we, as believers, have been programmed for a sudden departure.

Next, we will be together with our loved ones in the clouds. There is currently a great emphasis being placed on personal relationships. If we resist becoming more brother-related than God-related, this is a commendable Christian attribute. It is certainly reflective of a standard that will be part and parcel of our experience in heaven.

Much could be said about whom we wish to see and what we wish to say at the grand reunion of believers at the Rapture. My mind immediately goes toward my father, who led me to Christ, and to all of the things I did not tell him before he was suddenly snatched from our presence. I'm sure you have the same thoughts about those who are dear to you.

But perhaps, when we arrive, just being there with them will be enough. Just maybe, all that we have wished to say will already have been, in some way, conveyed before we arrive. Wouldn't that be wonderful?

What we do know is that we will be *together*—that's the operative word here—and that, with all of the warts removed, we will be together for all of eternity.

Oh, we can think of many problems. What about families broken by divorce? Or husbands and wives and this matter of death and remarriage? Well, we can say definitively that when we get home at last, we will enter the family circle that we have never fully known before. We have seen snatches of it here in the relationships we have experienced with our families. But in heaven, with Him, the concept of family extends to the entire body of Christ—not just one *body* but, surpassingly, one *family*. He will explain how it will all work out, but, nonetheless, *together* will be graced by a totally new dimension when we see Him.

Better yet, we will "meet the Lord in the air." Immediately, all of those thimble-sized questions will be answered once and for all. What does He look like? How old will He appear? And the like. At last—at long last— we will see Him. I suspect that when we do see our Lord, we will realize that we have had a pretty good look at Him all along. After all, He has left us a portrait of Himself in the Word. And the Spirit of God has superior powers of description.

But the desire, unequaled in the here and now, will be satisfied when our eyes behold him. I found it expressed admirably in the heart sounds from a black pastor, John Jasper, now gone from us for slightly more than a century.

In a sermon preached two weeks before he went home to heaven, the aged pastor took his congregation on a mind's-eye journey of his coming entrance into glory. His angel escort had some encouraging words.

"Now, Mr. Jasper, you can see all the folks you've preached about. Want to see Moses?"

Yes, he did want to see Moses. "But not now."

"Do you want to see Joshua, Caleb, David?"

"Yes, I want to see them all. But not now."

"How about John? Philip? The Ethiopian? The black Cross Bearer?"

"Yes, oh yes. But not now."

"Then who do you want to see?" asked his somewhat perplexed guide. "Your old mother, Tina? She's livin' in a great mansion now."

"Yes, I want to see my mother. She gave me to God before I was born, prayed me into glory when I was a wild, reckless boy. Prayed me into preachin' the gospel. Yes! I do want to see my mother. But not now."

"Well, John Jasper, who do you want to see here, anyhow?"

"Oh, Angel," the heaven-hungry preacher replied, "just lead me before the Great White Throne and let me gaze a thousand years into the face of my Jesus."[1]

Such are the longings of those who expectantly await seeing Him face to face.

Finally, "so shall we ever be with the Lord." How can we, who have been all our lifetimes bound by the limitations of time and space, grasp the reality of eternity?

Yes, we have read that with God, "one day is...as a thousand years, and a thousand years as one day" (2 Peter 3:8), but how can we really relate that to anything we have known? We, of course, cannot—and I think, at this point, that's for the better. We have a job to do, and it is a job that is clearly limited by time and opportunity. Better to press on and let all of our forever be tantalized by our expectation of what's ahead.

The Ultimate Comfort

"Wherefore, comfort one another with these words" (1 Thessalonians 4:18). That's the final word. To paraphrase Paul on another subject—that of the possession or lack of worldly goods—he said, "be...content" (1 Timothy 6:8). In whatever your state, learn to evoke an *it is enough* lifestyle.

He has not told us quite all we would like to know about the Rapture. But for now, we are comforted and content—it is enough.

The late Dr. J. Sidlow Baxter found himself in a dilemma over this matter of being taken in the Rapture or making his exodus through the door of death.

"I think," he said, "when all is said and done, that I would probably prefer dying to the Rapture."

My astonished reply was, "But why?"

"Well, Elwood, you see, if I go in the Rapture, you and everyone else will be there at the same time, and I'm sure it will take some time to have His attention. But if I die, I will have Him all to myself immediately. What do you think of that?"

I quite understand the tongue-in-cheek logic of Dr. Baxter's statement, although I opt for the Rapture myself. What I do know, because He told us, is *that, whether we wake or sleep, we should live together with him"* (1 Thessalonians 5:10).

Maranatha!

[1] *Rhapsody in Black*, Richard Ellsworth Day (The Judson Press, 1953), pp. 140-141.

Let that cry, "Behold, the bridegroom cometh,"
be continually sounding in your ears, and begin
now to live as though you were assured that this
night you were to go forth to meet Him.
                              —George Whitfield

Chapter Seven

THE TRIBULATION: JACOB'S TROUBLE OR THE CHURCH ON TRIAL?

"Antichrist Revealed!"

This is a headline you might expect to see on the front page of a tabloid displayed at a supermarket checkout stand. No doubt it has been used many times by journalistic purveyors of the sensational. Such statements are not, however, confined to secular organizations. Today it is increasingly common to read or hear claims of such "reve-lations" made by self-anointed prophetic "experts" who major in speculating about subjects that are obscure or are not specifically identified in Scripture. This is, of course, nothing new and, I might add, is something we shall see much more of as we progress into the last days. People—yes, even some Christians—seem to be drawn to hearing "some new thing." Thus, there is always enough of a mar-ket for the latest "revelation" to make it profitable to create another "authority" on prophetic themes.

Preparing the church to face the rigors of the Tribulation period, seeking signs, searching for the ashes of the red heifer and the ark of the covenant, checking on the devious intent behind every "666" license plate or road sign, and hosts of other available illustrations are theological novel-ties that illustrate the point just made. We are living in an age of what we might term "tabloid eschatology." Indeed, such speculative meanderings are becoming a kind of Christian cottage industry these days. Some of these mat-ters are of minor consequence—only serious if they distract some brethren from more important matters related to our great commission.

Among the long-standing favorites of those who deem it fruitful to delve into some of the mysteries of the Word is setting dates for the Lord's return or identifying the Antichrist. This has been going on for centuries, we know, but let us again be reminded that on both scores, those so sure that they have inside information from God on these matters have been universally wrong. With the year 2000 soon to be upon us, you can be sure that their tribe will increase, and a host of believers will be distracted from the purpose to which they are called. In addition, many will be ill-taught and thus equally ill-prepared for what is ahead. A most serious consequence of this endeavor is the loss of joy and expectancy over the imminence of our blessed Savior's return. This being true, it is incumbent upon us that we understand the vital nature of our mission in the last days and the promise of the blessed hope that is ever before us.

The Promise

Regarding the matter of the seven-year Tribulation period, during which God's wrath will be poured out on an unregenerate world, the church has an irrevocable promise from God. It is given to us repeatedly and in simple terms. I select only two of the many references that make the point. The first is 1 Thessalonians 1:10: *"And to wait for his Son from heaven, whom he raised from the dead, even Jesus, who delivered us from the wrath to come."* The "wrath" referred to here is divinely executed judgment that will be poured out during the seven-year Tribulation period.

A clear companion word comes to us later in the same epistle. Again speaking specifically in the context of the Tribulation, Paul says, *"For God hath not appointed us to wrath but to obtain salvation by our Lord Jesus Christ"* (1 Thessalonians 5:9).

Thus we are told that preparing for the Tribulation period is not to preoccupy believers in the last days. And we are not told to be on the lookout for the Antichrist. Those who are doing so are committing at least two major errors:

1. They are looking for the wrong person. We have been instructed, many times over, that we believers are to be *"Looking for that blessed hope, and the glorious appearing of the great God and our Savior, Jesus Christ"* (Titus 2:13).

2. In looking for and preparing to fight the Antichrist, believers are being turned from the blessed hope to a dreadful prospect.

We used to sing a little chorus that was a great comfort to God's people:

Turn your eyes upon Jesus, Look full in His wonderful face; And the things of earth will grow strangely dim in the light of His glory and grace.

Those simple words beautifully catch the essence of the church's hope. He is the object of our affection during our present pilgrimage. We are looking *unto* Jesus every moment of every passing day. At the same time, we are also looking *for* Jesus to come and call us to the place He is even now preparing for us. This is our blessed hope—it is ever before us.

Purged or Purified?

Some people are making the serious error of saying that the church must be taken through at least part of the Tribulation period in order to be purified and made fit for the presence of Christ. The idea is that the church is in such a sad spiritual state and has become so taken by the wiles of the world that it will be necessary for the church to suffer through enough of the trauma of the Tribulation to be purged and made fit for the presence of God.

While we quickly acknowledge that much of the church has strayed from the pathway of His purpose and is in need of correction, it is quite another thing to assert that, this being true, the church must suffer a sort of purgatorial purification by suffering His wrath.

A first question is obvious: When has the church, over the past 2,000 years, been collectively fit—or worthy, if you will—of the presence of Christ? The answer to that question is patently obvious: in terms of personal purity and self-originating worthiness—never. This is the crux of the problem posed by the idea of purging by Tribulation. The very thought calls into question the sufficiency of the cross work of Jesus Christ and actually places believers of the last days in a kind of double jeopardy.

The seven years of the Tribulation period is the time of the official outpouring of God's wrath. (For a detailed explanation of the seven years of wrath, see Dr. Renald Showers, *Maranatha: Our Lord, Come!*). For Christian believers, divine wrath has already been poured out—poured out on our Lord at the cross. There He suffered God's wrath and, according to Isaiah 53:5, *"with his stripes we are healed."*

Peter referred to this fact in his first epistle by saying, *"Who [Christ]...bore our sins in his own body on the tree, that we, being dead to sins, should live unto righteousness; by whose stripes ye were healed"* (1 Peter 2:24).

The extent of our healing is fully clarified in 2 Corinthians 5:21: *"For he hath made him [Christ], who knew no sin, to be sin for us, that we might be made the righteousness of God in him."*

The heart of our redemption is found in the fact that Jesus Christ, in His cross work, agonized under God's outpoured wrath in such a way that He paid in full the penalty for our sins. We are therefore no longer required to pay a debt that we could not pay. Indeed, Jesus has "paid it all." This is, of a certainty, why, when Christians die, they are taken immediately into His presence. There is no judgment for believers, no interim examination to see if we are worthy of entering His presence, and no purgatorial suspension. Our judgment took place two thousand years ago on a skull-shaped hill outside the old city walls of Jerusalem. Therefore, we are delivered into glory on the basis of the fact that we have trusted Christ as our personal Savior. It is His worthiness, not ours, that is at issue in whether we are fit for release in death or the Rapture when He comes for His saints.

Jacob's Trouble, Not the Christian's Trial

A basic problem with people who are committed to the idea that the church will pass through the whole, or at least a portion of, the Tribulation period is a lack of understanding of the divine purpose for the Tribulation. The church has no mission to fulfill during that time. In other words, the church of Jesus Christ is irrelevant to the purpose of God on earth during the seven-year Tribulation period.

Whenever the church and Israel are confused or their programs are intermingled, there is likely to be confusion about some central factors involved in that brief but excruciating time.

The "great multitude, which no man could number, of all nations, and kindreds, and peoples, and tongues" of Revelation 7:9 is often confused with the church. These people are, however, identified specifically as "they who came out of the great tribulation, and have washed their robes, and made them white in the blood of the Lamb" (Revelation 7:14). Their coming out of the Great Tribulation has nothing to do with the Rapture. These are Tribulation saints coming in a procession created by martyrdom and passing into the presence of the Lord and the "elders" (representatives of the church), who are already there. In fact, one of the elders poses the question, *"Who are these who are arrayed in white robes? And from where did they come?"* (Revelation 7:13).

The mercy of God, who in every dispensation would have "all men to be saved" (1 Timothy 2:4), is magnified in these blood-washed Tribulation saints. They are, in a sense, the final gleanings before the great second advent coming of our Lord, and we can be eternally grateful that His mercy reaches even into the agonies of the Great Tribulation. These people represent gleanings because this body is not emblematic of the thrust of what God purposes in the Tribulation period. Those seven years, in their entirety, are given to three great themes— themes that must be grasped in order to understand what He is doing during this brief but climactic time.

What are the threefold central segments of the Tribulation period?

1. The national reconciliation of Israel
2. Crushing Gentile belligerence
3. Revealing the Son from heaven

The key to the entire matter is Israel. The Tribulation period is, in a very real sense, the time of Israel's consummating visitation. Several indicators point to Israel as the main element in the Tribulation period.

Jeremiah 30:7 says this: "Alas! for that day is great, so that none is like it; *it is even the time of Jacob's trouble.*" Note, please, that this period is designated as "the time of Jacob's trouble," not the church's trial. In Daniel 9, the premier prophetic passage in the Bible, we find that in the final week of the 70-week prophetic scenario, the Antichrist will sign a seven-year covenant with the nation of Israel, but in the middle of that week he will break his agreement (Daniel 9:27).

When the infamous "abomination of desolation" (Matthew 24:15) is set up by the Antichrist, it will be erected in the Temple courts in Jerusalem. "Who [the Antichrist] opposeth and exalteth himself above all that is called God, or that is worshiped, so that he, as God, sitteth in the temple of God, showing himself that he is God" (2 Thessalonians 2:4).

Jerusalem will be the focal point of activity in the Armageddon phase of the last battles. The city will become "a cup of trembling": "Behold, I will make Jerusalem a cup of trembling unto all the peoples round about, when they shall be in the siege both against Judah and against Jerusalem" (Zechariah 12:2).

From these texts and scores of others, it is clear that Israel, Jerusalem, and the Jewish people are the focus of the program. But to what purpose? Two portions of Scripture reveal a glorious end.

Romans 11:26 makes a concise, clear statement regarding God's intentions for Israel: *"And so all Israel shall be saved; as it is written, There shall come out of Zion the Deliverer, and shall turn away ungodliness from Jacob."*

Israel will come to a day of national reconciliation with their long-estranged Messiah. It will not be an imposition of salvation on the nation against its will. Nor is there any hint that Jewish people will be saved by another covenant and therefore need not respond to Jesus as Messiah/Savior. Not at all. The basis of the national reconciliation spoken of here is Israel's Armageddon cry for the Messiah to come.

> And I will pour upon the house of David, and upon the inhabitants of Jerusalem, the Spirit of grace and of supplications; *and they shall look upon me whom they have pierced, and they shall mourn for him, as one mourneth for his only son, and shall be in bitterness for him, as one that is in bitterness for his firstborn* (Zechariah 12:10).

The second major passage on Israel and Jacob's trouble outlines the agonizing process that will bring the Chosen People to the end of their own resources and cause them to cry out for Him. It is found in Zechariah 13:8-9.

Before we examine Israel's pathway to reconciliation, let us quickly scan the entire process as revealed in Zechariah 13 and 14. There is no better example of the threefold purpose of the Tribulation than is found in this strategic passage.

1. Israel's reconciliation: Zechariah 13:8-9
2. Crushing Gentile belligerence: Zechariah 14:1-3
3. Revealing the Son from heaven: Zechariah 14:4-5

Israel's Reconciliation

"And it shall come to pass that in all the land, saith the
LORD, *two parts in it shall be cut off and die; but the third part*
shall be left in it" (Zechariah 13:8).

Israel's final Holocaust is depicted in these verses.
Satan's last attempt to annihilate the Jewish people comes
into view in a few terse words. A fuller explanation is given
in Revelation 12, which tells of Satan's unrelenting fury
unleashed in view of his knowledge that his time is coming
to an end. "And when the dragon saw that he was cast unto
the earth, he persecuted the woman [Israel] who brought
forth the male child [Christ]" (Revelation 12:13).

This is the final act of a story that has unfolded across the
centuries.   Memories flood the mind: Herod the Great
slaughtering the innocents in Jewish Bethlehem in an attempt
to kill the newborn King; mad Adolf Hitler's satanically driven "final solution" to the Jewish problem; and, closer to the
present, the frantic terrorist attempts to annihilate the State of
Israel and kill Jewish people.

To us, it all may seem like a disjointed patchwork of
senseless brutality, and in a way it is. But from Satan's
perspective, there is a reason behind his persistent
attempts to wipe out Jewry. We will do well to remember
that all anti-Semitism, wherever it crops up, is directly
related to this diabolical program. You see, the Jewish
people possess a great wealth of promises from God. A
land, a kingdom, and a divine destiny are all etched in the
granite of His Word. Israel's reconciliation to the Messiah
is the center pole of this program. Simply put, Satan is
attempting to destroy the Chosen People before the nation

can embrace the Messiah and live out its destiny. Thus, fully two-thirds of the people in Israel will perish during the trauma of the Tribulation.

But the emphasis does not rest on this depressing note. This is not the end of the story. There is a last word on the matter, and it comes from the God who has promised the preservation of Israel and its people.

> *And I will bring the third part through the fire, and will refine them as silver is refined, and will test them as gold is tested; they shall call on my name, and I will hear them. I will say, It is my people; and they shall say, The LORD is my God* (Zechariah 13:9).

When we wonder how it is all going to turn out—what with kamikaze suicide bombers and entrenched enemies promising to end it all for the nation of Israel—the final word is here. The last act will usher in Israel's golden era. "And they shall say, *The LORD is my God!*" It is the proverbial light at the end of the tunnel.

Crushing Gentile Belligerence

International Gentile hostility toward God and His program on earth reaches as far back into the mists of antiquity as the opening chapters of the Book of Genesis. As a matter of fact, the Babel experience is cited immediately before the record of God's call to Abram.

> And the whole earth was of one language, and of one speech. And it came to pass, as they journeyed from the east, that they found a

plain in the land of Shinar; and they dwelt
there. And they said one to another, Come, let
us make brick, and burn them thoroughly. And
they had brick for stone, and slime had they for
mortar. And they said, Come, let *us* build *us* a
city and a tower, whose top may reach unto
heaven; and let *us* make *us* a name, lest we be
scattered abroad upon the face of the whole
earth (Genesis 11:1-4).

Babel was the threshold of the great house of Babylon and
the system that has endured to defy God. It will continue to do
so until it is crushed by the Lord Jesus in the climactic confrontation of the last days.

The words *us* and *we* dominate the text. This is
mankind's grand attempt to shake themselves free of
divine sovereignty. The great difference between what is
demonstrated here and the attitude of Abram expressed in
the next few verses is that Abram was listening to God;
these people were not.

The marks of their rebellion are very clear:

  • God wanted them to scatter and populate the earth;
  they said, "No!" They sought unity without being subject to deity.

  • "Let *us* make *us* a name" says that they also sought
  prosperity without depending on the Lord's benefi-
  cence. They wanted to achieve prosperity through
  independent means.

  • Their little tower of Babel, designed to be a gate-
  way to the heavens, speaks loudly of their desire to
  worship according to their own will—lift them-

selves up by their own bootstraps. Babel presents a vivid case of religion without acknowledgment of their creator and sustainer.

This is the basis of the Gentile system that has plagued the earth from that day until this. We should not, therefore, be surprised to hear trumpeted in our ears themes of a new age, global economic unity, and recognition of all religions. The problem for such "one world without God" devotees, however, is that they and their Babylonish system are on a collision course with the Almighty.

The flames of Babylon's destruction are seen in Revelation 17 and 18. The focal point is set forth in the summary Tribulation text we are following in Zechariah 14.

Gathering the Nations

The time is the conclusion of the Tribulation period. The nations are assembled in the climactic "Day of the Lord" confrontation. It is the day toward which all of history is running with increasing velocity. Jerusalem and the Jewish people are the central factor, both in what God is doing and in what Satan is attempting to counteract.

Behold, the day of the LORD cometh, and thy spoil shall be divided in the midst of thee. For I will gather all nations against Jerusalem to battle; and the city shall be taken, and the houses rifled, and the women ravished; and half of the city shall go forth into captivity, and the residue of the people

> shall not be cut off from the city. Then shall
> the LORD go forth, and fight against those
> nations, as when he fought in the day of bat-
> tle (Zechariah 14:1-3).

All of the nations of the world will come to the stage for the last great battle between God and those who defy Him. The emphasis is upon *all*, which answers the oft-posed question about just where the United States will be when this action takes place. *All* of the nations, under the leadership of the Antichrist, will assemble to attack Jerusalem and its Jewish inhabitants.

We have seen, in our consideration of Zechariah 13:8-9, why Satan is obsessed with wiping out the Jewish people. The Jews are the People of the Book—the people of the promises. Thus, God will step in to secure their salvation as a national entity.

This is an equally important parallel to the process that has a direct bearing on some intriguing events leading up to the gathering against Jerusalem. It is the central feature in the transcending strug-gle between Satan and Christ.

Before the battle for the Holy City is joined, the Antichrist will make a visit. It is described in 2 Thessalonians 2 and embellished for detail in Revelation 13 and Matthew 24.

"Who [the Antichrist] opposeth and exalteth himself above all that is called God, or that is worshiped, so that he, as God, sitteth in the temple of God, showing himself that he is God" (2 Thessalonians 2:4).

The Antichrist in the Tribulation Temple in Jerusalem? Showing himself to be God?

Why?

Why would the leader of a Gentile system that is opposed to all that God and Jerusalem stand for go there to announce his claim to deity?

Furthermore, he comes as one whose very person and deeds are "after the working of Satan with all power and signs and lying wonders, And with all deceivableness of unrighteousness in them that perish" (2 Thessalonians 2:9-10).

The Antichrist is a product of the western confederation of nations. Daniel 7 marks his rise as coming from the "fourth kingdom"—that is, the revived Roman Empire. The Antichrist will reach the height of his power during the last half of the Tribulation period, which will be marked by his opposition to God as "he shall speak great words against the Most High" (Daniel 7:23, 25).

Obviously, he is not a Jew but a Gentile. If he is going to claim divinity, as did the Roman emperors of old, why not make his announcement in Rome? It would be an impressive backdrop for such a display. Or why not in Brussels, where the European Economic Union is headquartered? Why not in New York, at the United Nations? These are all prominent centers of Gentile pride and power.

But no. Instead, he comes to Jerusalem, and for a very simple reason. Jerusalem is the place of the throne from which the Messiah is destined to reign in righteousness for a thousand years.

"The LORD also shall roar out of Zion, and utter his voice from Jerusalem, and the heavens and the earth shall shake; but the LORD will be the hope of his people, and the strength of the children of Israel" (Joel 3:16).

Jerusalem is the place to which Jesus Christ promises to return. Thus, Satan and his counterfeit Christ will attempt to seize the throne before the King can arrive and take His rightful place as King of reconciled Israel and ruler of a subdued world.

The one who reigns is at the heart of the struggle for Jerusalem, and understanding this will clarify why there is so much fuss and fury made over the place. None of the past and present moves toward a humanly achieved "peace process" will succeed. This struggle is between God and Satan—between light and darkness—and it will be settled only when He comes.

Behold, He Cometh With Clouds

There is a marvelous verse in the Book of the Revelation that says so well what generations of believers have longed for in their hearts.

"Behold, he cometh with clouds, and every eye shall see him, and they also who pierced him; and all kindreds of the earth shall wail because of him. Even so, Amen" (Revelation 1:7).

This verse embodies the thrust of the Revelation. It is not the revelation of Saint John the Divine. It is the glorious revelation of Jesus Christ—the Messiah of Israel and sovereign Savior of all who will believe in Him.

This is made clear in Revelation 1:8. Who is the coming one who will be seen by "every eye"?

"I am Alpha and Omega, the beginning and the ending, saith the Lord, who is, and who was, and who is to come, the Almighty."

The Scripture speaks eloquently here and says all that needs to be said. But all readers must be aware of the awesomeness of His coming and flee to the arms of a loving Savior while there is yet time.

Our central verse on this subject, however, is Zechariah 14:4. It is the third clarification of the purpose for the Tribulation period. First, you will remember, was the reconciliation of the nation of Israel. Second was the crushing of Gentile belligerence. Third, and the purpose now before us, is the revelation of God's Son from heaven.

> *And his feet shall stand in that day upon the Mount of Olives, which is before Jerusalem on the east, and the Mount of Olives shall cleave in its midst toward the east and toward the west, and there shall be a very great valley; and half of the mountain shall remove toward the north, and half of it toward the south...and the* LORD, *my God, shall come, and all the saints with thee (Zechariah 14:4-5).*

This is the grand answer to the simple question Jesus' disciples asked at least two millennia earlier: "Lord, wilt thou at this time restore again the kingdom to Israel? And he said unto them, It is not for you to know the times or the seasons, which the Father hath put in his own power" (Acts 1:6-7).

They were instructed not to speculate about the time of His coming but to make His name known to the ends of the earth. They were to rest in the promise of His return. That promise was reiterated by the attending angels as He ascended back to heaven.

> And while they looked steadfastly toward heaven as he went up, behold, two men stood by them in white apparel; Who also said, Ye men of Galilee, why stand ye gazing up into

heaven? *This same Jesus, who is taken up from you into heaven, shall so come in like manner as ye have seen him go into heaven* (Acts 1:10-11).

And when that great day of His glorious, "every eye shall see him" coming dawns, where will those early believers— and all of the rest of us who have trusted Him as Savior and Lord through the centuries—be? Zechariah says that when the Lord God comes, "all the saints" will appear with Him (Zechariah 14:5).

What a stunning revelation. When "the LORD [goes] forth...as when he fought in the day of battle" (Zechariah 14:3), we will be with Him. When His feet touch down on the Mount of Olives in Jerusalem, we will be with Him. When the mountain splits in two to prepare a gathering place for the judgment of the nations, we will be with Him. And when He mounts His throne to begin a reign of one thousand years of millennial bliss, we will be with Him.

"And the LORD shall be king over all the earth; in that day shall there be one LORD, and his name one" (Zechariah 14:9).

And where will we be? "They shall be priests of God and of Christ, and shall reign with him a thousand years" (Revelation 20:6).

How much better can it be? These most wonderful truths make our "little trials" seem as nothing, make the shadows flee away, make the hope that is ours shine all the more brightly.

"Even so, come, Lord Jesus" (Revelation 22:20).

The dynamic of this new life is the expectation of the coming of Jesus Christ. When a royal visit is expected, everything is cleansed and decorated and made fit for the royal eye to see. The Christian is the man who is always prepared for the coming of the King of kings.

—William Barclay

Chapter Eight

WALKING IN THE NEW CREATION

Jesus shall reign where'er the sun,
Does his successive journeys run;
His Kingdom spread from shore to shore,
Till moons shall wax and wane no more.

The throes of the Tribulation period fade with the brightness of the Lord's Second Coming. The long-awaited Millennium that follows will bring with it the peace that has eluded humanity since Cain killed Abel in the first act of violence to strike the human family. Both the creation and the redeemed who enter this era will breathe a collective sigh of relief at the absence of Satan, nature's being subdued, and the reality that Christ has taken His throne in Jerusalem. Isaiah wrote of the day with a sheer beauty and unmistakable clarity. We sing of it, long for it—but the prophet adds the dimension that makes the heart leap with anticipation.

> The wolf also shall dwell with the lamb, and the leopard shall lie down with the kid; and the calf and the young lion and the fatling together, and a little child shall lead them. And the cow and the bear shall feed; their young ones shall lie down together. And the lion shall eat straw like the ox. And the nursing child shall play on the hole of the asp, and the weaned child shall put his hand on the adder's den. They shall not hurt nor destroy in all my holy mountain; for the earth shall be full of the knowledge of the LORD, as the waters cover the sea (Isaiah 11:6-9).

It will be a glorious time, the like of which we have never seen before.

1. Christ will be on His throne, ruling from Jerusalem.
2. Saints will rule with Him, as He directs.
3. Redeemed Israel will live out the promises made to Abraham.
4. Peace, justice, and equity will rule the day.
5. The animal kingdom will no longer kill to survive.
6. A Millennial Temple will stand on Mount Moriah in Jerusalem.
7. Gentile nations will come annually to the Temple to keep the Feast of Tabernacles.

Isaiah adds further details describing the situation for reconciled Israel and life in the Millennium.

> And I will rejoice in Jerusalem, and joy in my people; and the voice of weeping shall be no more heard in her, nor the voice of crying. There shall be no more in it an infant of days, nor an old man that hath not filled his days; for the child shall die an hundred years old....And they shall build houses, and inhabit them; and they shall plant vineyards, and eat the fruit of them....They shall not labor in vain, nor bring forth for trouble; for they are the seed of the blessed of the LORD, and their offspring with them. And it shall come to pass that, before they call, I will answer; and while they are yet speaking, I will hear (Isaiah 65:19-24).

His thousand-year reign will be the first installment in the eternal program planned for those who know and love Him.

What we have seen, however, must not be confused with what eternity holds for believers. There are some rather sharp distinctions, namely in the Millennium:

1. Unsaved people will be present.
2. Death will still plague people born in the Millennium.
3. There will be the need for personal salvation.
4. The period will close with an uprising against Christ led by Satan, who will be "loosed [from his prison] a little season" (Revelation 20:3).

Although blessing and bliss will be hallmarks of the Millennium, mankind's sinful nature and disposition will still be factors to be dealt with.

The Final Test

There has been considerable speculation about why, after living in an environment blessed by the visible presence of God Himself and virtually perfect surroundings, a rebellion will be raised as the Millennium draws to a close. The rebellion will be a solemn chronicle of how far humanity has fallen.

> And when the thousand years are ended, Satan shall be loosed out of his prison, And shall go out to deceive the nations which are in the four quarters of the earth....And they went up on the breadth of the earth, and compassed the camp of the saints about, and the beloved city; and fire came down from God out of heaven, and devoured them (Revelation 20:7-9).

It is important to know that the rebels will not be from among those who enter the era as redeemed people—that is, the saved of the Tribulation period who are alive at His return in glory. Nor will they be those previously raptured from the church age, who will be reigning with Him during the thousand years. We do not face the dismal prospect of becoming lost a second time. In Christ we possess eternal life. In fact, we are as saved at this moment as we will be when we've been in heaven for 10 trillion years.

Rebels will be drawn by Satan from among those who, in spite of all that the Millennium offers, still refuse God's grace and mercy. The fact that they will join the Devil in his last manic attempt to defeat Christ is evidence that fallen humans are, indeed, as depraved as the Word of God declares them to be.

I have met many people over the years who say that it is because of the evil, suffering, and inequities all about them that they do not trust Christ and become believers. If they could only witness, in tangible form, the goodness and mercy of God, they say, they would believe. During the Millennium this excuse will be taken away. It will be emphatically demonstrated that by the close of the thousand-year reign, humanity will have been tested under every conceivable condition—*Innocence* (Genesis 1:28), *Conscience* (Genesis 3:7), *Human Government* (Genesis 8:15), *Promise* (Genesis 12:1), *Law* (Exodus 19:1), *Grace* (Acts 2:1), and the *Kingdom* (Revelation 20:4)—yet, in the end, failure to meet the divine standard will rule the day. The fact that "The heart is," as Scripture tells us, "deceitful above all things, and desperately wicked" (Jeremiah 17:9) will have been established as irrefutable and become an important issue to be faced at the Great White Throne Judgment.

When the Nations Bow Down

From north to south the princes meet
To pay their homage at His feet;
While western empires own their Lord,
And savage tribes attend His word.

We were created to worship. Accordingly, every human being will bow before a master, good or evil, because it has been programmed into the heart of mankind by God. This compulsion places an impassable gulf between us and the animal world. For this reason, advocates of the New Age will never successfully bring men and women to the same level as beasts, or elevate animals and their environment to equality with men and women created in the image of God (Genesis 1:26).

One of the foremost elements of the Kingdom will be the ascent of the nations of the earth to Jerusalem to worship. If they refuse to come, dire consequences will result. Can you imagine the scene in and around Jerusalem as national leaders and common folk stream into the city from every corner of the globe? It will be a total reversal of the Armageddon experience, when "all nations" (Zechariah 14:2) will gather together against God, His Christ, city, and people.

> And it shall come to pass that every one that is left of all the nations which came against Jerusalem shall even go up from year to year to worship the King, the LORD of hosts, and to keep the feast of tabernacles. And it shall be that whoever will not come up of all the families of the earth unto Jerusalem to worship the King, the LORD of hosts, even upon them shall be no rain (Zechariah 14:16-17).

Foremost in the worship of the Millennium will be the presence of God in the midst of His people. Ezekiel tells us that the Shekinah glory that filled the inner court of Solomon's Temple will return to His house during the thousand-year reign. "And the glory of the LORD came into the house by the way of the gate whose prospect is toward the east....and, behold, the glory of the LORD filled the house" (Ezekiel 43:4-5). His presence in Jerusalem will assure Israel and remind the nations that His people have been reconciled and the day of the New Covenant has dawned.

The question must be asked, What will be the manner of worship at the Millennial Temple? The reinstitution of sacrificial worship has troubled many. Why, after Jesus made the final sacrifice and the Temple was destroyed, will the Lord mandate the construction of another Temple and order sacrificial worship to begin, as described in Ezekiel 40 through 44? At the heart of the festive gatherings are the sacrifices.

"And thou shalt give to the priests, the Levites, who are of the seed of Zadok, who approach unto me, to minister unto me, saith the Lord GOD, a young bullock for a sin offering" (Ezekiel 43:19).

Although few would venture to say that they have a simple answer to the question, we can gather some strong inferences.

The sacrifices will be memorial in nature. These offerings will not remove sin, any more than did the sacrifices under the Mosaic Law. Those offerings looked forward to the coming of Christ. In the same way, offerings at the Millennial Temple will look back on the finished work of Christ. The offerings will replace the communion service, which will not be practiced during that period.

Thus, offerings will be made in the same sense as they were in the Old Testament. In the Millennium, however, they will be a powerful testimonial to the fact that a blood offering is no longer needed for sin. Christ made the last sin offering, once for all, on the cross.

In this regard, we recall that there will be great hosts of unsaved people living at that time. The sacrifices will undoubtedly serve as a clear witness for Christ. In other words, Temple worship during the Millennium will be God's grand object lesson for those who need salvation.

Serving from the Heart

Were the whole realm of nature mine,
That were a present far too small;
Love so amazing, so divine,
Demands my soul, my life, my all.

If the presence of the Lord in the Shekinah glory and the person of the reigning Messiah is the center pole of the Millennium, the next most compelling factor is the heart service rendered by reconciled Israel and the church.

One of the most beautiful passages of Scripture in the
Old Testament reveals the New Covenant that God promises the sons of Abraham. It is specifically for Israel and has
not been taken from them and given to the church. Notice
the specific language that the Holy Spirit chooses.

> Behold, the days come, saith the LORD, that I will
> make a new covenant *with the house of Israel, and
> with the house of Judah,* Not according to the
> covenant that I made with their fathers...*But this
> shall be the covenant that I will make with the house
> of Israel* (Jeremiah 31:31-33a).

It is as though God anticipates the theological folly that will, centuries later, claim that God's covenant promises to Israel have been
withdrawn and given to the church. He insists that such is not the
case! Israel will have her promises, and a new heart to receive them.

> After those days, saith the LORD, I will put my
> law in their inward parts, and write it in their hearts,
> and will be their God, and they shall be my people.
> And they shall teach no more every man his neigh-
> bor, and every man his brother, saying, Know the
> LORD; for they shall all know me, from the least of
> them unto the greatest of them, saith the LORD; for I
> will forgive their iniquity, and I will remember their
> sin no more (Jeremiah 31:33b-34).

Perhaps you have observed what I have observed among Jewish
people. Some seem to be intellectually convinced of the true identity of the Messiah. I have one very good friend who believes it
all: the virgin birth, the miracles, even the resurrection. But he
stumbles over the deity of Christ. That vital key has not yet been
turned in his heart. I find this particularly true to one degree or
another with a number of Israeli tour guides. They know more

about the New Testament than some pastors seem to, and their love for the land and their people cannot go unnoticed. One thing alone seems to be lacking: true faith in the Messiah. When it is accomplished—when the heart-key is turned—I can visualize a great army of people serving the Lord with unbridled enthusiasm. Such will be the case when the Millennium arrives. If the reconciled Jewish remnant serves the Lord with a determination equal to the resistance to the gospel that their reluctant brothers and sisters showed in the days of their rejection of the Messiah, we must believe that they will turn the world upside down for Christ.

Also serving in the Millennium will be the body of Christ, the church. Having returned to the earth with the Lord at the close of the Tribulation period, the saints are destined to reign with him. "Blessed and holy," He says, "is he that hath part in the first resurrection; on such the second death hath no power, but they shall be priests of God and of Christ, and shall reign with him a thousand years" (Revelation 20:6).

What will we do? That's an extremely important point. But He chooses not to tell us. The Apostle Peter calls us "a chosen generation, a royal priesthood, an holy nation, a people of his own, that [we] should show forth the praises of him who hath called [us] out of darkness into his marvelous light" (1 Peter 2:9).

How this "holy nation" will serve in concert with His chosen nation is not revealed. Suffice it to say that our reign will be glorious!

Payday

There will come a time when the Devil has had his day and he will plague the presence of the saints no more. At the conclusion of the thousand-year Millennium, that great day will come. For Satan and his dark-hearted, angelic co-conspirators and nefarious fallen human cohorts, payday will arrive. In what is revealed in rather rapid-fire succession, three events will take place: Satan will lead a last rebellion; he will be cast into the lake of fire; and the judgment of the Great White Throne will take place. It is almost as though God wants to get these dreadful events out of the way so that we can all move on to better things.

Satan's final assault against Christ can be described as being aborted by fire. After gathering numbers of rebels "as the sand of the sea" (Revelation 20:8), he will move against "the camp of the saints" (Revelation 20:9), which is, of course, Jerusalem. This time, however, there will be no flight from the city, no ravishing of women, no host of martyred saints. It seems that the cup of God's patience will be filled to the brim, and His response will be appropriately swift and decisive. Omnipotence will deliver the final *coup de grace.*

"And they went up on the breadth of the earth, and compassed the camp of the saints about, and the beloved city; and fire came down from God out of heaven, and devoured them" (Revelation 20:9).

From the destruction of the last army, things will move quickly to the disposition of the satanic problem. He will be— without judicial review—cast into the lake of fire.

"And the devil that deceived them was cast into the lake of fire and brimstone, where the beast and false prophet are, and shall be tormented day and night forever and ever" (Revelation 20:10).

No need for a trial—only an execution carried out. The Devil was tried and convicted before humanity ever came on the scene. In a manner of speaking, his final attempt for a self-created reprieve was foiled when Christ died on the cross and exited the tomb, in spite of all that Satan could do to keep Him inside. His subsequent rampage across the centuries that followed were, in the final analysis, his trek to the execution chamber, which in this case is described as the "lake of fire."

For your comfort and mine, the words that should arrest our attention are "forever and ever." This is not an interlude, such as will be the case during the Millennium when Satan is bound for a thousand years. Incarceration for eternity is the word here. We will never again be cursed by the presence of our great arch foe. And the echo reverberates across the eons: *Never again! Never again! Never again!*

For a satisfying comparison, we need only look at John 14:16. Here we are informed of the length of the Holy Spirit's stay in believers. "And I will pray the Father," Jesus says, "and he shall give you another Comforter, that he may abide with you *forever.*" He will dwell with us for as long as God has promised us life in Christ—for eternity. For a like span of time, the Devil will be off the scene. World without end, amen!

Finally, the rest of the dead—all unsaved—will be brought to the Great White Throne.

> And I saw a great white throne, and him that sat on it, from whose face the earth and the heaven fled away, and there was found no place for them. And I saw the dead, small and great, stand before God, and the books were opened; and another book was opened, which is the book of life. And the dead were judged out of those things which were written in the books, according to their works" (Revelation 20:11-12).

The object of this judgment is not to determine whether a person is saved or lost, but rather to determine the degree of punishment to be faced in eternity. That will be determined by their works—how much light from God was spurned, how many opportunities to receive the gospel message were refused, how much influence from godly saints was brushed aside, etc.

The key to this judgment is found in the "book of life." There are no names of the lost to be found there. It stands as a mute witness before them—a devastating testimonial of their refusal to trust Christ as their personal Savior. When the book is closed, "whosoever was not found written in the book of life was cast into the lake of fire" (Revelation 20:15).

Without question, this somber event brings a pall of sadness over the hearts of those of us who know the Lord. In our mind's eye we can see the faces of friends and loved ones who, insofar as we can determine, never trusted Christ. Three considerations can help sustain us. First, we have no way of knowing, short of eternity, whether they, in fact, died lost. We will be surprised to meet many in glory whom we had not expected to see there. Then, we must realize, difficult as it may be for us to comprehend, that no one will be in heaven who does not want to be there. No forced conversions will be imposed on those who choose to live and die lost. Finally, the most assuring word can be found in an encounter from the Book of Genesis. Abraham was interceding for Sodom and imploring the Lord to spare that most wicked of places for the sake of the righteous people found there. As he grasped for words to express his anguish, he blurted out what he knew to be true: "Shall not the Judge of all the earth do right?" (Genesis 18:25). He will.

All of the shaded mysteries that are veiled to our finite minds we commit to the competence of the God to whom we've committed the safekeeping of our souls—we rest in Him.

Home At Last

Picture Abraham standing beneath the Middle Eastern night sky, looking up at a sea of stars extending to infinity in all directions.

WALKING IN THE NEW CREATION   137

"And he [God] brought him forth abroad, and said, Look now toward heaven, and count the stars, if thou be able to number them: and he said unto him, So shall thy seed be" (Genesis 15:5).

Abraham was seeing more than stars, however, for he was a man with eternal vision. He was looking beyond the stars for a more enduring promise than land, a seed, or a covenant. Abraham was a man who was looking for a city—an eternal city—beyond the shores of this world shackled by time. Hebrews 11:10 details his heart-hope.

"For he looked for a city which hath foundations, whose builder and maker is God."

Abraham was not alone in his longing for that better land. Among the multitude of companions in the faith named in Hebrews 11 were,

> These [who] all died in faith, not having received the
> promises but having seen them afar off, and were
> persuaded of them, and embraced them, and con-
> fessed that they were strangers and pilgrims on the
> earth. For they that say such things declare plainly
> that they seek a country...now they desire a better
> country, that is, an heavenly; wherefore, God is not
> ashamed to be called their God; for he hath prepared
> for them a city (Hebrews 11:13-16).

He shared the common lot of believers in all generations who have the sense of being but pilgrims and strangers in this world—tent dwellers, if you will. I don't know how it is with you, but I increasingly feel that the convulsions of our planet—morally, politically, and environmentally—are harbingers of the demise of this little speck in the universe that we call Earth.

But it is not as though we were not forewarned. Second Peter 3:10 says that "the heavens shall pass away with a great noise, and the elements shall melt with fervent heat; the earth also, and the works that are in it, shall be burned up."

The timing of this seems to be implied in Revelation 20:11. While the judgment of the Great White Throne is taking place, we find "the earth and the heaven fled away" from the face of the Lord who occupies the throne. Perhaps this fleeing is the conflagration promised by Peter.

At any rate, as the description of the Great White Throne Judgment comes to a close, we are immediately introduced to a spectacular view of the new heaven and the new earth.

"And I saw a new heaven and a new earth; for the first heaven and the first earth were passed away, and there was no more sea" (Revelation 21:1). Our first glimpse of the new heaven and the new earth emphasizes the word *new*. No less than four times in the first five verses of Revelation 21 we are face to face with the word *new*. It is an impressive encounter: a *new* heaven; a *new* earth; a *new* Jerusalem; and all things made *new*.

All things *new*! The new creation in which we will walk throughout all eternity is overwhelming evidence of the depths of God's love for us. His purpose was not just to win a resounding final victory over Satan, but to share "a place prepared" with the redeemed forever.

Have you noticed that God has programmed into human beings a love for new things? While the desire for new things can become a distraction, there is no doubt that possessing something new has a special place in our hearts.

We see this manifested from earliest childhood. Before my granddaughter was a year and a half old, she was assisting her mother in the selection of new garments. She is nearly three now, and her list of desires for new apparel increases by the day. It's the same for most children—and adults. The smell of a new car, a new house, a new baseball glove, or a multitude of other new things impacts us in positive ways. Again, this is because God has placed within us an inherent attraction to new things. The consummate fulfillment of such God-given desire will be found in the new heaven and new earth in store for believers.

The New Jerusalem

"And I, John, saw the holy city, new Jerusalem, coming down from God out of heaven, prepared as a bride adorned for her husband" (Revelation 21:2). The new Jerusalem will be beautiful beyond description. Its very dimensions are staggering. The city will be a full 1,500 miles square and 1,500 miles high, with foundations of precious stones. Its gates will be graced with the names of the twelve tribes of Israel. This city will need no light from the sun or the moon. The new Jerusalem will be the Temple of God, and He will give us His light. The gates of the city will be perpetually open, and God's glory will be brought into it. Also, "the nations of them who are saved shall walk in the light of it, and the kings of the earth do bring their glory and honor into it" (Revelation 21:24). This Jerusalem, literally the city of gold, will be the dwelling place of the saints for all the endless ages of eternity.

I am fascinated to find descriptions of conditions there that embody many of the things with which we are most familiar here on earth.

    1. His people will be there (Revelation 21:3). In other words, we will be at home with the family. Did it ever strike you that we are learning at this moment, here on earth, the language of the family that we will use forever. We speak eas-

ily of our brothers and sisters in the faith. We have been taught to call God our Father.

2. The Tabernacle of God (Revelation 21:3), although different by heavenly proportions, is something we have been associated with since being taught of it in our Sunday school days.

3. God's throne will be there (Revelation 22:1). His throne, before which we have lingered in intercession and agonized in our grief, will be central to the city and the scene.

4. It will be a literal new creation, a world prepared by God (Revelation 22:1-2), reminiscent of the one we share now—but unsullied by the curse.

5. There will be a system of national entities, with godly kings who will bring their glory into the new Jerusalem.

6. The "water of life" (Revelation 22:1), of which all believers are partakers since the day when Jesus first invited us to come and take of the water of life, will be there.

7. The "tree of life" (Revelation 22:2), a constant testimonial to the life we have in Him, will be there. It will be a reminder of what we have found, to replace what our first parents so tragically lost in the Garden of Eden (Genesis 3:22).

8. Jerusalem will be the shining city of our new home (Revelation 21:10)—Jerusalem of gold, the city that brings joy to believers. Perhaps this is why, even today, Israel's Jerusalem beckons us back and captivates our hearts.

9. Best of all, in addition to the Father, the Lamb will be there (Revelation 21:22). That's how we saw Him first and have known Him best—as "the Lamb of God, who taketh away the sin of the world" (John 1:29).

Therefore, with all of the stunning beauty of the new creation and Jerusalem prepared for us, we will be at home in that wonderful place—home at last! This may be why, in the hearts of small children, there is such buoyancy when they sing:

> Heaven is a wonderful place
> Filled with glory and grace.
> I want to see my Savior's face.
> Heaven is a wonderful place.

Heaven is a place prepared for us. But, in a very real way, we are a people whose hearts are being prepared in the here-and-now for our home in the by-and-by.

Absentee Heartaches

"And God shall wipe away all tears from their eyes; and there shall be no more death, neither sorrow, nor crying, neither shall there be any more pain; for the former things are passed away" (Revelation 21:4).

For me, this passage speaks volumes. Perhaps it is because, as a pastor for nearly a quarter of a century and then spending years so near the horrors of the Holocaust, I've seen far too many broken hearts and shattered lives. But one day—let's pray it will be soon—safely home and resting at His side, the flow of tears will cease, and sorrow will be no more.

Think of it. Imagine excising from your life all of the tears, treks to the graveside, crying out of the agonies of a broken heart, and every pain that has ever touched you. Suddenly all are removed. That's what is in store for us, beloved friend. The thought evokes a doxology to the incomprehensible God who stooped so low in order to lift us so high.

His Servants Shall Serve Him

It's all so familiar, yet it seems to escape us somehow. A few thoughts back, I asked the question, What will we do in the Millennium? You will remember that the answer was, We are not told. That should be enough to satisfy us at the moment. But the question pops up again here, as we look ahead into the eternal state.

A phrase in Revelation 22:3-4 speaks volumes. "And there shall be no more curse, but the throne of God and of the Lamb shall be in it, and his servants shall serve him; And they shall see his face...."

"His servants shall serve him."

For eternity we will be commissioned to do whatever He bids us. This, after all, is the essence of the commission that we were given two thousand years ago. That commission was rather more focused than this one. It was to make His name known—to proclaim the gospel. Now we are informed that our mission will be to serve Him in the simplicity of what He commands. At the outset of this volume, I talked of the simplicity of most things that He commands us to do, things we often complicate beyond recognition.

"His servants shall serve him." How simple the words, but how profound the prospects. Just trust and obey, do what you're told, but, in the process, you are a workman under God, impacting eternity. We considered earlier some of the things to be found in heaven that will have a familiar look or ring to them. Here again, we come face to face with a familiar theme: service for the Master. The fact is that we will be doing in heaven precisely what we are to be doing here: serving the Savior with our whole hearts.

If you want a preview of the eternal workplace, I have a suggestion. Look into the eyes of a small child when he or she is given a small task to perform by a parent or grandparent. The sparkle of anticipation and eagerness to swing into action is something many of us adults have lost. Again, watch the glow of satisfaction when the child returns with the words, "Mission accomplished!" I'll guarantee that the words "Well done" or a small reward could not be more appreciated by an adult receiving the highest honor our nation can bestow. And that, after all, is the wonder of serving the Lord: giving all we have to hear His "Well done."

Going Home

In the end, I find that a discussion of heaven is more easily given to matters of the heart than to theological dissection. There are very good reasons for this. Heaven fits into the same category as the situation faced by Jesus' disciples when they were told that He was going away. They needed something they could grasp in the depths of sorrow or, perhaps better said, something that could grasp their hearts in their time of need.

I think that is where many of us find ourselves today. Have you noticed that people who sing the simple old gospel songs—music for the heart—are making a remarkable comeback these days? Some may say that this is due to the demoralizing state of some of our contemporary Christian music. This may be part of it. But think of the subjects of much of the old music. These people are singing about triumphing over death, the resurrection morning, great gatherings in glory, the Rapture of the saints, and the like. Theirs are songs to lift the spirit and urge people on the way.

In this environment, when we are being hammered by Satan and the forces of evil as never before in our lifetimes, maybe a good look at the heavenly streets and the home He is preparing for us is not such a bad thing.

Our conclusion is that we will soon be home and that each of us can be grateful to a caring God who has so clearly mapped the way for us by giving us His Word. For believers, there should be no surprises—only recognition of the signposts marking the way until we are called away.

Whatever comes, what should be our attitude toward it all? Suffer me to quote once more from the words of a great black preacher who leaped from the shackles of slavery into the sheltering arms of a delivering Christ. John Jasper had faithfully preached the gospel for some 40 years or more after the close of the Civil War. It was said of the preacher that "It was not to Jasper's taste to argue on heaven as a doctrine. With him it was as if he were camping outside of a beautiful city, knowing much of its history and inhabitants, and in joyous expectation of soon moving into it" (*John Jasper*, by William E. Hatcher, Christian Book Gallery, St. John, Indiana).

When, at 89 years of age, John Jasper mounted his pulpit for the last time, he said, "My words are for my brethren, my church. They are the people for whose souls I watch. For them I will stand and report at the last day. They are my sheep, and I am their shepherd, and my soul is knit with them forever." And then, as if looking over into the forever he had spoken of, and expecting a momentary departure, he declared, "I am now at the river's bank and waiting for further orders."

Let this be our attitude in these last days: watching for the souls of men while we stand at the river's bank—"waiting for further orders."